A TAOIST TRADER

Vadym Graifer

Published by RealityTrader Services.

ISBN 978-0-9737796-5-3

Printed with CreateSpace.com

Typeset in *Aver* at SpicaBookDesign
www.spicabookdesign.com

For complete list of RealityTrader products and courses,
please visit www.realitytrader.com

Philosophy is just so much nattering unless you also use what you discover as a ground for being.

~ D. Gerrold

About This Book

Let us start with a few questions.

Should you decide to become an engineer and design bridges – will the first question you ask be "Where do we put piles in the river's bottom?"

Should you decide to become a surgeon and perform heart surgeries – will the first question you ask be "Where do we make the first cut?"

Should you decide to become a pilot and fly 747 – will the first question you ask be "Which switch do we flick first?"

Didn't think so. You will study the principles of design first, to learn how to build bridges. You will learn how the human body works, to understand the illnesses and cures. You will study how the planes work, to learn to operate them. You will also study how the subject of your occupation interacts with an environment – bridge with its load and elements, body with tasks of daily life, plane with atmospheric phenomena.

Seems obvious enough, right? Well, the first question most aspiring traders ask is "Where do we enter and exit our trades?" For some reason, the necessity to study what market is, how it works, what forces move it, how to read their actions, and how to act to achieve success in trading escapes beginner traders, as if it were understood by anyone by default.

Listen to the conversation of two beginners, and the majority of their discussion will be particular stocks or sectors, entries and exits. Listen to the conversation of two traders who survived their first 3 to 5 years, and you will hear very different topics discussed – market philosophy and traders' psychology. Listen to the conversation of two traders having 15 and more years of trading under their belts, and you will find them discussing... well, dinner menu most likely; their views on the market's inner workings are likely to be, for all practical intents and purposes, similar.

For as long as I have written about markets and trading, I have emphasized trading philosophy and psychology. **Techniques of Tape Reading** devotes the whole first part of the book to this topic; **The Master Profit Plan** starts with a "Trading Philosophy" chapter. For a long while I was looking for the best and most practical way to describe the inner workings of the market and a trader's behavior in it. The answer dawned on me during a discussion with a good friend and fellow trader Mark ("nemo.") Trained in the arts and philosophy of an ancient discipline, and seeing parallel ideas in my writing, he saw it fitting (and I am very grateful he did) to introduce me to that philosophy.

Enter the Tao.

According to the philosophy, Tao is the ultimate origin of all things, physical and metaphysical, that operates through principles that can be observed in the world around us. Tao is a law according to which everything happens. Call it Laws of Nature; call it set of rules; call it natural patterns, or call it guiding spirits – whatever your concept for it is, everything we observe is a manifestation of the Tao and functions according to its rules. Yes, that means you and the markets too.

The classic text of Taoism is the Tao Te Ching, written by Lao Tze about 2500 years ago, and is the second most translated book in the world. The book consists of 81 short poems. There is no direct way to accurately understand their meaning, for a few good reasons. The poetic form does not easily lend itself to strict logical concepts and concrete interpretation. The author had not intended the meaning to be easily understood. Finally, translation from Chinese is a subject of interpretations, and a translator without subject matter expertise (in this case without a Taoist master) is prone to error. For the purposes of this course we are using the translation by Lin Yutang; most importantly, for interpretation, we use the excellent works by Grand Master Alex Anatole, The Truth of Tao and The Essence of Tao. By no means should this course be considered the work by which to study Taoism. This is a book applying the Taoist philosophy to trading – for a more comprehensive explanation and understanding of Taoism I'll direct you to the aforementioned books and Alex's site http://www.tao.org/. The books unfold this amazingly pragmatic philosophy in a logical and elegant way. The reader will undoubtedly be fascinated by the direct practical applications, clarity and delicious paradoxes of the Taoist way of thinking.

Every chapter in this book consists of three parts.

First (in ***bold italic***) is a poem from the Tao Te Ching. We used 44 chapters in this book. 27 of them are the main poems describing vital principles; 17 are supplementary, providing a somewhat different angle, new detail or a refresher.

The second part (in *italic*) is an explanation of the poem's basic meaning taken from the works of Grand Master Anatole. Corresponding parts of the poem are recited for clarity. Make sure to read it with great attention. Taoist thinking is not immediately obvious; it relies on paradoxes and is expressed in a way that requires a certain mental adjustment. You will be amazed to see how the meaning of the seemingly vague words turns around and become stunningly clear – when you start thinking as a Taoist.

The third part (in normal font) is the trading application. This is where we turn philosophical abstractions into practical application. What the market is. What your place in it is. What forces move it. How they act. What their motives are. How to read their intentions. How to act to stay safe and profit from the action. How to condition your mind to act in a disciplined cold-blooded fashion. Taoist principles create the canvas that we use to combine these concepts and beliefs in a clear well-structured trading philosophy that governs your actions and gives you inner strength to follow the right course.

Going from chapter to chapter, you will encounter some themes more than once. Some of them are only touched briefly in early poems and expanded in greater details later. Some of them are combined to show their interaction. Some are shown from different angles to demonstrate how they influence various aspects of market action. Don't rush through the chapters – soak the content in, let it blend together. Gradually, you will sense a whole new outlook being formed; no side of the market will be seen as standalone – instead, it will all come together in amazing clarity. Read the course carefully and apply it methodically – and many confusing aspects of market events will become clear. You will find yourself having unambiguous recipes for your own actions and the ability to follow them with resolve and discipline.

The book addresses three major aspects of trading:

- Understanding the inner workings of the market
- Understanding thought process and guiding emotions of other traders
- Understanding and controlling your mindset and actions

Last comment before moving to the book itself: do not take it as stiff dogma. You may find different analogies or applications for some of the Taoist principles, or think of something better suited to your particular situation. Taoism is nothing if not flexible, and Tao is bigger than any of us. As long as you comply with natural laws, such modifications constitute finding your own niche and can only be commended.

Table of Contents

Prologue

Below is the last poem of Tao Te Ching. Please read it and try to "sense" its meaning. Please spend some time, contemplating it unhurriedly.

81. The Way of Heaven

True words are not fine-sounding;
Fine-sounding words are not true.
A good man does not argue;
he who argues is not a good man.
the wise one does not know many things;
He who knows many things is not wise.
The Sage does not accumulate (for himself).
He lives for other people,
And grows richer himself;
He gives to other people,
And has greater abundance.
The Tao of Heaven
Blesses, but does not harm.
The Way of the Sage
Accomplishes, but does not contend.

Chances are you feel the power and poetic beauty in the words; however the logic and actual application of them feels elusive and difficult to grasp.

When you are done reading the book, return to this page once again and re-read the poem. The meaning of each word and each line will be incredibly clear to you. Where did the vagueness go? The raw power and amazing clarity will be palpable; some words will have a meaning that is totally opposite to what you perceived before going over the book. The perfectly completed cycle of returning to the first page upon finishing won't escape you either.

This is but one small measure of how much you have learned. Your trading performance will be another. Yet another is a balanced stress-free way in which trading becomes incorporated in your life.

On to the book.

1.
On the Absolute Tao

The Tao the can be told of
Is not the Absolute Tao;
The Names that can be given
Are not Absolute Names.
The Nameless is the origin of Heaven and Earth;
The Named is the Mother of All Things.
Therefore:
Oftentimes, one strips oneself of passion
In order to see the Secret of Life;
Oftentimes, one regards life with passion,
In order to see its manifest forms.
These two (the Secret and its manifestations)
Are (in their nature) the same;
They are given different names
When they become manifest.
They may both be called the Cosmic Mystery:
Reaching from the Mystery into the Deeper Mystery
Is the Gate to the Secret of All Life.

This poem describes one of the cornerstones of the Taoist philosophy. It states that the source of all phenomena cannot be fully understood by the human mind. We can observe only the manifestations of this source, of the law governing all things. We must accept, and understand there are limits to what we can know. Understanding the border between what we know, and what we think we know is crucial. It represents the border between reality and fantasy – a border we cross much more often than we think.

The Tao the can be told of
Is not the Absolute Tao;
The Names that can be given
Are not Absolute Names.
The Nameless is the origin of Heaven and Earth;
The Named is the Mother of All Things.

As a manifestation of the Tao, we must accept our inability to comprehend the source of all creation. Nor can we define Tao in our language – defining A by differentiating it from B would diminish Tao to A or B, while true Tao is a source of both A and B, therefore is bigger than A or B. This reduces our role to observers of the manifestations of Tao.

Such limitation should not be lamented though. It leaves us in position to analyze what can be verified by practical application, leaving aside what is beyond our comprehension.

Therefore:
Oftentimes, one strips oneself of passion
In order to see the Secret of Life;
Oftentimes, one regards life with passion,
In order to see its manifest forms.

Society subjects us to indoctrination by communicating certain values and beliefs from birth until death. Such beliefs forced upon us may not, and often don't, reflect the true nature of things; neither do they necessarily result in behavior that serves our best interests.

In order to observe the undistorted reality, one must be able to suspend those lifetime beliefs. As we "strip ourselves of passion" (remove our ingrained emotional attachments) in order to approach the matter analytically, we can study the visible manifestations of Tao. As we understand them, we apply our passion to actions guided by beliefs that more closely reflect reality.

These two (the Secret and its manifestations)
Are (in their nature) the same;
They are given different names
When they become manifest.
They may both be called the Cosmic Mystery:
Reaching from the Mystery into the Deeper Mystery
Is the Gate to the Secret of All Life.

The invisible source, the Tao, expresses itself in visible, material manifestations. To begin to understand its workings, we must study those manifestations.

Taoism pursues simplicity, trying to strip away the complexities of the "deeper mysteries." Taoist principles seem counter-intuitive at first, mostly thanks to our predetermined ideas and limited intellects. The more we apply Taoist concepts in practice though, the more natural and profound the knowledge becomes. Simple and profound knowledge can be applied in practical ways. A robust system of beliefs leads to clarity. Clear understanding of reality forms the recipe for correct action. Correct action leads to contentment, the Taoist definition of success.

The Tao the can be told of
Is not the Absolute Tao;
The Names that can be given
Are not Absolute Names.

IT is of paramount importance to understand and accept the concept that it is **impossible** to know all the information related to market movements. This is a cornerstone to understanding the market and the nature of trading. The idea that it is possible and necessary to know all the information about ongoing and intended transactions by all market participants leads to endless frustration. The notion that one must possess all the information is a misconception inevitably leading to erroneous conclusions and incorrect action.

Let's look deeper into this concept. Is it really possible to know everything about all the plans of all the market participants? Do they themselves know what they are going to do all the time? None of the plans are absolute; they are rather varied responses to different events and developments. While every market participant does, or at least should, plan his actions, he also has, or should have, contingency plans. No one knows the future, thus a good trader plans for deviations. Therefore, instead of a single plan he has a "tree" of possible scenarios and responses. The important conclusion for us to draw from this is: since each player has no definite plan for his actions, it's impossible to "know" or somehow figure out with certainty what is going to happen.

The notion that any kind of analysis, whether fundamental, technical, or a combination thereof, can give us an accurate prediction of future events, is mistaken. Let's test the assumption that such predictions are possible through a thought experiment.

Let's assume that you researched in great detail a certain company and came to a conclusion about what is going to happen to its stock. Your findings are positive, and you are certain that the price is going to rise. Next, imagine a big fund manager making a decision to re-allocate his investments to pursue some different lucrative opportunities, thus selling his holdings in the stock on which you are focusing. Obviously such actions will create selling pressure in it for totally unrelated, and most importantly, unforeseeable, reasons. If that is not enough, envision a big holder of the stock being hit with legal and emotional complications of a sudden divorce, thus liquidating his holdings in your stock. Clearly, none of those events have anything to do with company prospects, industry developments or any kind of chart indications. No mortal can possibly foresee such developments. Now, to make the case stronger yet, let's envision that somehow you've managed to compile information allowing you to conclude that there are presently, let's say three large players selling out their positions and seven more that are holding theirs, and you even found out the size of their holdings. Such information goes well beyond what is practically impossible ever to discover, but even that is not going to be enough to create absolute certainty. Is it really possible to forecast whether they still remain holders if the price doubles tomorrow? Or drops fifty percent? As you can see, this is a highly liquid situation where intentions are not only practically impossible to discern but also are continuously subject to change driven by unforeseen and unexpected events.

What will happen to a trader who insists on "knowing it all" before making his trading decision? Such a trader, highly influenced by his training in previous professional endeavors, would have a hard time committing to any action before he "knows." His endless research would take him to endless new layers of information where each new piece may easily contradict that which was previously gathered, making his task practically impossible. Alternatively, he may exhaust the means of obtaining new information. At this point he will face two choices. First is total paralysis – lack of "necessary" information will leave him incapable of taking action. Second, is to continue gathering information beyond all reasonable means, and inevitably fall victim to misinformation. This will happen because:

- When all reasonable sources of information are exhausted, the vast field of false knowledge, wild assumptions and unfounded theories start;
- In this state of eagerness for any information we tend to be especially gullible as we strive to fill the informational void and lower our protective barriers.

In the end our trader will finally find himself badly confused and misinformed. His course of action based on misinformation is likely to be incorrect and to put him on the losing side of the trade.

All this takes us to an extremely important conclusion that will profoundly influence our entire trading approach.

The market is an uncertain environment which works in probabilities.

This concept is not really shocking if you think of the market being a part of life. After all, in every days life we encounter uncertainty all the time; we don't know with certainty what is going to happen. Our plans get altered or ruined constantly, and people and natural elements around us often act quite unpredictably.

We, however, tend to think of trading as a profession rather than a life process, and professional training is structured in a way that makes us think in certainties rather than probabilities. Our training in professional fields is usually certainty-oriented. We are taught to gather all the information and calculate the definite outcome of our decisions. The market, however, is not of concrete or steel construction. Rather it's an amalgamation of people and organizations making decisions, thus its behavior is the sum total of human behavior. As such, it's far from being definite, or completely rational – just like life itself. Failure to appreciate this difference creates a conflict that needs to be resolved, before the trader can become consistently successful in the market.

The only resolution that creates a robust foundation for correct action is acknowledgement and acceptance of uncertainty in the markets. This acceptance prepares us for learning to act with certainty in an uncertain environment. Again, this is not a totally foreign skill for us – we deal with some level of uncertainty on a daily basis in all walks of life. In order to apply our natural skills in trading though, we need to unlearn some of the beliefs instilled in us during our professional training; we also need to acquire a certain mindset that would make us well adjusted to functioning in an uncertain environment. Only then will we be able to observe accurately the manifestations of market information through tape action (by the tape we mean price and volume). Such manifestations will add the necessary bits and pieces to what we know about a particular stock or sector, allowing us to verify our assumptions and work out the correct course of action.

Such an approach streamlines our decision-making process making it pragmatic and sensible. The first step in this process is information gathering. Second step is verification through observation– simply speaking, watching the market action for confirmation of what we think we've learned. At this point we will see one of two possible scenarios.

- If we see confirmation, our trading idea is validated and we can act on it. In practical terms, if what we learned about the company or gained from analyzing the chart is positive and the tape action is bullish, we have our confirmation.
- If the market action invalidates our information, this divergence in and of itself presents a great trading opportunity. If what we know about the company is positive and this seems to be the generally accepted opinion, yet market action is bearish, there is a strong possibility of the information being incomplete, false, having no relation to price action or being fully priced in. Acting against such information is a genuine acceptance of the principle "All information about the market can not be known." Using practical manifestations to verify the information and to determine our course of action is the most powerful weapon giving the greatest probability of putting you on the right side of the trade.

Our beliefs formed in the process of gathering information all too often become associated with our ego. We tend to view confirmation of our conclusions as proof of our self-worth. This creates an emotional attachment to our ideas, and as a result of such emotional investment we lose our objectivity. The desire to be right distorts our perception of reality. This is where Taoism's advice to "***strip oneself of passion***" comes to help. If you sincerely accepted the impossibility of knowing everything about the company or chart you research, and the impossibility of predicting market movement with full certainty, you no longer gauge your self-worth by the results of your predictions. In fact, you do not even predict – you simply execute the best course of action and let the market take its course. In the process you continue monitoring market action to ensure that the manifestation (market action) matches your understanding. If you see a deviation, you have no problems correcting your actions since there is no ego involved.

Ego and emotional involvement triggered by lack of understanding and acceptance of this principle manifest themselves in various ways. One of the most frequent and deadly manifestations for a trader is a failure to apply a stop loss. A Taoist Trader who genuinely accepts the concept of the market working in probabilities will have no problems to take his loss while it's small as soon as the market's action invalidates his trading idea. If, however, this concept is not ingrained in a trader's mindset, he is likely to insist on being right in a vain attempt to validate his ego by being above the probabilities.

We see here how such a global concept leads us to a very practical conclusion and set of actions. We started with a wide philosophical concept and arrived at a mindset constituting the dream of every trader – being a detached observer, seeing reality clearly and capable of actions free of emotions.

2.
The Rise of Relative Opposites

When the people of the Earth all know beauty as beauty,
There arises (the recognition of) ugliness.
When the people of the Earth all know the good as good,
There arises (the recognition of) evil.
Therefore:
Being and non-being interdepend in growth;
Difficult and easy interdepend in completion;
Long and short interdepend in contrast;
High and low interdepend in position;
Tones and voice interdepend in harmony;
Front and behind interdepend in company.
Therefore the Sage:
Manages affairs without action;
Preaches the doctrine without words;
All things take their rise, but he does not turn away from them;
He gives them life, but does not take possession of them;
He acts, but does not appropriate;
Accomplishes, but claims no credit.
It is because he lays claim to no credit
That the credit cannot be taken away from him.

When the people of the Earth all know beauty as beauty,
There arises (the recognition of) ugliness.
When the people of the Earth all know the good as good,
There arises (the recognition of) evil.
Therefore:
Being and non-being interdepend in growth;
Difficult and easy interdepend in completion;
Long and short interdepend in contrast;
High and low interdepend in position;

Tones and voice interdepend in harmony;
Front and behind interdepend in company.

A foundation principle of Taoism is that of Oneness. Every phenomenon consists of opposites bound together as a single unified whole. The Tao pairs light with shadow, night with day, and life with death. In social norms, beauty co-exists with ugliness, good with evil, fair with unfair. One can not exist harmoniously without the other; one can not be recognized without the other. Beauty could not be seen and recognized if it were not for ugliness providing the standard to measure against. How could one understand heat without understanding cold? How could one recognize light without knowing darkness? The relation of opposites is one of cause and effect. They originate from the same source. They balance each other, complement each other, add to each other, depend on each other and complete each other.

Therefore the Sage:
Manages affairs without action;
Preaches the doctrine without words;

Understanding the way opposites relate should naturally lead the individual to adopt the principle of non-interference and emotional non-involvement. In other words, we should not impose our values, our likes and dislikes on the natural order of things. Artificial and subjective values contradict the objective rules of nature. Our ideas of the "right way" are irrelevant to an impartial Tao. Instead of attempts to apply such ideas, Taoism advises us to accept the natural flow and harmonize our thinking and behavior with it. Such harmony can be achieved by observance and acceptance without grading things as good and bad; without taking sides; and without positioning oneself with one part of the phenomenon against the other.

All things take their rise, but he does not turn away from them;
He gives them life, but does not take possession of them;

The duality and oneness of opposites means constant rotation, never-ending change. A Taoist does not fight or reject change, he adapts to it. Encountering an obstacle, he does not resent it – he deals with the impact, producing the most fortuitous result possible.

He acts, but does not appropriate;
Accomplishes, but claims no credit.
It is because he lays claim to no credit
That the credit cannot be taken away from him.

"He acts but does not appropriate" *means that in the process of adaptation a Taoist does not fixate on any single result as the ultimate measurement of his success or failure. He realizes that a constantly changing environment will inevitably lead to some of his attempts failing. By accepting such failures in advance he liberates himself from a depressed state of mind caused by negative outcomes.*

Continuous change also means that victories will inevitably be followed by defeats. A Taoist claims no fame, avoiding arrogance. He accepts good times and expects bad times to come. When they do, he will be ready to adjust.

Concepts of Oneness and Opposites are illustrated by the Yin/Yang symbol known throughout the world for 2500 years.

Yin and Yang affect one another and keep one another in place. The symbol represents the duality of all phenomena where opposites are seen as opposing manifestations of the same principle. Each side, black and white, represents a polar opposite and is given equal weight, symbolizing the harmonious proportions of the natural phenomena. A rotating pattern between the two colors suggests continuous waxing and waning between the opposites. The small dot of the opposite color within each area symbolizes the presence of the opposite in each phenomenon – there is some light in the night just as there are shadows in the daylight, thus no phenomenon is absolutely pure.

When the people of the Earth all know beauty as beauty,
There arises (the recognition of) ugliness.
When the people of the Earth all know the good as good,
There arises (the recognition of) evil.

Therefore:
Being and non-being interdepend in growth;
Difficult and easy interdepend in completion;
Long and short interdepend in contrast;
High and low interdepend in position;
Tones and voice interdepend in harmony;
Front and behind interdepend in company.

THE concept of Oneness and the relation between Opposites manifests itself in practically every aspect of the market. One of the most fundamental changes in the market is the shift from bull phase to bear phase and back. Every buyer becomes a potential seller at the moment he initiates his long position. Thus, a bull market from its very beginning carries the seeds of the future bear market. Each of them has their time, their place and their role. Bull markets increase valuations, bring profits to investors and shower companies with additional capital. In the process, two things occur "under the hood": as life becomes easier and easier, excesses appear and blossom. Companies tend to spend freely, to hire excessively and to become reckless; investors tend to throw caution to the wind and traders tend to underestimate risk; more and more buyers enter the market, increasing the number of potential sellers and gradually tipping the balance in favor of a future downward move.

Finally, at some point, the bear market arrives. Its role is to clean the excesses of the bull phase. As the market drop eats into investors' profits, they start withdrawing capital. The companies start tightening their belts. Those companies that overextended themselves beyond repair go bankrupt. Those that managed themselves more wisely turn leaner and meaner and eventually come out of the rough times stronger. Investors become much pickier; traders control their risk much more tightly. Those who don't adapt to the change lose their capital and exit the game.

Now, let's see what happens as a bear phase develops. All those who sold their positions turn now into potential buyers. Those who sold the market short become future buyers as well. Investment capital avoids the dropping market and waits on a sideline. Meanwhile, the natural selection process described in the above paragraph occurs and separates the winners from losers among the companies. Future candidates emerge for that waiting capital to pounce on. This selection warrants more effective application for the investing capital. In other words, the bear market carries the seeds of the future bull market in it – just as the bull market contained the future bear. This rotating pattern, the constant rebalancing and presence of the opposite in each side are the perfect manifestation of the Yin and Yang.

Therefore the Sage:
Manages affairs without action;
Preaches the doctrine without words;
All things take their rise, but he does not turn away from them;

Understanding and accepting the relationship of opposites is necessary to find the right way to act when changes occur. Without such understanding, emotional involvement will cloud judgment; labeling the phenomenon as good and bad and taking sides will occur, resulting in incorrect and unnatural behavior. Governments will meddle in the process of selection, saving losers from bankruptcy and punishing winners in the process. Such intrusions will diminish the effectiveness of investing as capital flows won't go to the most deserving areas, industries and companies. Investors taking sides by considering a bear market as "bad" will avoid seeking new opportunities as the bear market runs its course. Traders assuming that "markets are supposed to go up" will feel that shorting is unnatural for them and will refrain from it, forfeiting profitable opportunities.

Astute traders will be sensitive to the upcoming changes. They understand that every phase is not going to run forever. They will monitor the market for signs the movement is becoming excessive and risk rising beyond acceptable levels. Being free from emotional involvement frees their minds and senses, allowing them to remain detached observers. Not being committed to any direction, they initiate long and short positions with equal ease. They maintain their balance and remain in tune with market.

He gives them life, but does not take possession of them;
He acts, but does not appropriate;

Avoiding emotional involvement is equally necessary in order to remain objective about any given company or trade. "Falling in love" with a certain company leads to losing one's objectivity in decision-making. A trader has difficulty letting go when the facts contradict his conviction. This results in holding losing positions instead of cutting the loss while it's small. Similarly, being emotionally attached to a certain trade keeps a trader in the market even though the action tells him to close his position.

A trader that deeply understands the concept of Oneness, of relative opposites and constant change, understands and accepts one of the most vital concepts of trading: **losses are unavoidable and in fact constitute a necessary component of trading.** No trader in history avoided losses; and none ever will. Since the market is an uncertain environment that works in probabilities, some trades will be losing ones no matter how perfect a trader or his trading system. A trader must understand and accept it – then he will take his losses easily and cut them short. Refuse to accept this, and your losses will grow much bigger than they should, and eventually will overwhelm your wins.

Just as the Sage from the Taoist poem, a wise trader does not interfere with natural market flows. He does his best to be in tune with the market and align his actions with its currents. He makes no effort to force his opinion on the market; instead he observes the events unfolding and identifies them. As he recognizes what's happening, he makes sure that his position matches the market action as he understands it. At the same time he does not stay with his opinion forever – he continuously observes the market and has no difficulty re-aligning his positioning if developments do not confirm his opinion or if there is a change in the market's course (**He gives them life, but does not take possession of them**). Being free of emotional attachment to his opinion, a trader develops a high sensitivity to such changes.

Accomplishes, but claims no credit.
It is because he lays claim to no credit
That the credit cannot be taken away from him.

A Taoist Trader does not claim credit for winning trades, nor does he wallow in desperation over losing ones. Since he does not attribute wins to his genius, he has no need to attribute losses to his stupidity. Such an approach allows him to maintain emotional balance, without either elation or frustration. Understanding that trade results do not reflect on his personality establishes an emotional buffer between him and his trading. Such a buffer enhances his objectivity and helps him maintain the position of a detached observer. He doesn't experience emotional impulses stemming from a suffering ego. Such impulses make an emotional trader initiate trades based on his personal needs, desires and fears, not in the market's action.

Contrast this approach with one of a trader who elects to claim credit for each win, assigning it to his outstanding abilities rather than to a disciplined, principled methodology. Making any profitable trade his personal win, "***appropriating it***" he automatically makes any loss personal as well. This view triggers his ego involvement; a win becomes the subject of bragging and a loss becomes the source of emotional pain. His ego demands that he does not take losses; in vain attempts to avoid the unavoidable he is likely to hold losing position or start averaging down. The emotional balance is lost; the situation becomes personal, and his actions become irrational.

An astute trader does not focus on any single trade result, rather viewing his trading as a continuous process. Such an approach adds to his previously mentioned ability to feel at ease accepting a loss on any given trade. This again ensures that no loss gets out of hand; our trader keeps his losses acceptably small, not letting them grow uncontrollably and threaten his trading account.

Faithful to his understanding of Oneness/Opposites principles, a Taoist Trader understands that periods of wins will be followed by periods of losses; uptrends will be interrupted by pullbacks; downtrends will be interrupted by bounces; bull markets will result in bear phases which will lead to new bull stages. Accepting all these changes as natural, inevitable and welcome, he stays sensitive to and prepared for them.

Understanding the principle of Oneness and Opposites will also help you distinguish a real market guru from a questionable one. If you see a market commentator touting his winning calls without as much as an admission of losing ones, you know that you're dealing with self-promotion rather than with truth.

3.
Action Without Deeds

Exalt not the wise,
So that the people shall not scheme and contend;
Prize not rare objects,
So that the people shall not steal;
Shut out from sight the things of desire,
So that the people's hearts shall not be disturbed.
Therefore in the government of the Sage:
He keeps empty their hearts
Makes full their bellies,
Discourages their ambitions,
Strengthens their frames;
So that the people may be innocent of knowledge and desires.
And the cunning ones shall not presume to interfere.
By action without deeds
May all live in peace.

This poem contains a series of warnings against the popular values pushed upon an individual by the societal structure. To perceive reality objectively and free oneself from external influences, one must realize their danger to one's best interests. Many things promoted by the society as desirable, and by extension, adopted by the individual in fact have a hidden catch, leading to a downfall down the road. Over-accumulation of material possessions while sinking in debt is a glaring example of overextending oneself and assuming unnecessarily large risk. Thus, a Taoist constantly asks himself whether the things he sets out to acquire satisfy his real needs or the desires of his mind. He is cautious about getting himself into something, knowing that it is much harder to get out of it. Unrealistic desires are the illusions that distort the perception of reality.

*"**Keeping empty**" one's heart means to stay free from the values implanted from the outside. Taoist keeps an open mind while remaining skeptical. "Empty heart" doesn't mean he is void of values; His core values reflect the principles of the Tao. To "**make(s) full their bellies**" again refers to keeping the desires realistic. Instead of desiring to consume everything in sight, the belly enforces limits to what you need.*

A Taoist deploys an effective technique to understand differences between wants and desires. This technique is to imagine a perfect day, one that he could and would want to live for the rest of his life. Once such a vision of the perfect day is created, it provides a measuring stick for assessing where he is in respect to that goal.

"Discourages their ambitions" *means getting a realistic perspective on one's abilities, learning to work with the talents you have been given, rather than pursuing unrealistic goals. By checking your ambitions, you are less likely to become frustrated and bitter.*

"Strengthens their frames;

So that the people may be innocent of knowledge and desires" *means working on better understanding the solid Taoist principles. By remaining "innocent of knowledge and desires," Taoist rejects the artificial values designed to distort natural behavior. He realizes that following those, he would most likely act against his own interests.*

"And the cunning ones shall not presume to interfere" *– by the "cunning ones" Taoism means the social architects who try to impose their plans and ideas on the masses. Their actions are usually masked by the noblest intentions. This reference also includes those who try to outsmart reality believing that they can control an unpredictable future. The Taoist is not seduced into believing the promises set forth by society.*

"Action without deeds" *means to ingrain Taoist principles into one's mindset to such degree that they become an integral part of character, automatically resulting in correct behavior. The Taoist reacts to situations as they present themselves. He does not try to predict the future, understanding that anything can happen. Such an approach rids him of worries about his predictions coming true. His peace of mind stems from knowing he reacted to events according to sound, robust Taoist principles and not conforming to "good deed" as defined by society.*

Exalt not the wise,
So that the people shall not scheme and contend;
Prize not rare objects,
So that the people shall not steal;
Shut out from sight the things of desire,
So that the people's hearts shall not be disturbed.

The market environment has a high noise to signal ratio – the "noise" consists of propaganda and misinformation. Some is produced out of ignorance and some by design. Opinions, notions and beliefs are pushed upon the trading and investing masses by entities with agendas or without real knowledge. Some market commentators, driven by ego, are engaged in self-promotion. Others serve certain interests and promote them by talking "their book" through strategic talking points. It is imperative for a trader to see through these agendas and focus on the "signal" – the true information.

There are two possible approaches for a trader to deal with external noise. One is to block it off completely and trade solely off the market action. Such an approach is appropriate for short term trading mostly and can be somewhat limiting.

Another is to use the information flow as a measuring stick for the market action, find the divergences and use them as trading ideas. The underlying concept for such an approach: when there is a contradiction between the information and market action, the market action will always be the right answer. Seeing such divergences, a trader knows that either propaganda or ignorance is being pushed upon him. Taking the side of market action, he positions himself in accordance with reality. This approach offers great potential for profitable trades; as a trade-off it requires more experience and highly honed market observation skills when deciphering the incoming information and comparing the two. We will return to this concept in later chapters as it is one of the cornerstones of the market dynamics.

Often a beginning trader takes the information offered by market commentators at face value. As he progresses, he tends to start tuning it out; finally as his skills grow even further, he becomes proficient in spotting the divergences between information and price action. Finally he gains a critical mass of knowledge of a number of standard situations (repeating patterns), so he becomes capable of forecasting them in advance. Understanding how the propaganda machine operates helps him to form expectations of what kind of divergence is likely to appear. Observing the unfolding events, he finds his trading opportunity if his expectations are confirmed.

Examples of such divergences are:

- stock's failure to move higher on an upgrade or lower on a downgrade;
- market's failure to move higher on positive economic indications or lower on negative ones;
- prices' failure to move higher on widely expected positive news or lower on widely expected negative one.

Such divergences are especially effective in introducing a trading opportunity when they occur after an extensive move in the direction indicated by the news event. Thus, upgrade after a pronounced upward move and failure to make new high after an upgrade can be a powerful reversal signal.

Listening to chatter around the market events, a Taoist Trader will keep an open mind so he can appreciate valid comments and put them to a good use. He remains skeptical so he can spot an agenda or ignorance. He observes the market action and compares it to the comment's content so he can verify his assumptions and spot a trading opportunity should it present itself.

Therefore in the government of the Sage:
He keeps empty their hearts
Makes full their bellies,
Discourages their ambitions,
Strengthens their frames;
So that the people may be innocent of knowledge and desires.
And the cunning ones shall not presume to interfere.
By action without deeds
May all live in peace.

A Taoist Trader "***keeps empty his heart***"- doesn't allow himself to be influenced by someone else's trading decisions, other trading systems, or someone's fears and hopes. There is always some trader all too willing to argue his point of view. There are boards, forums and chats providing all kinds of "insight", reasonable and not so reasonable. Whether those expressing their opinions know what they are talking about or not, their approach, circumstances, objectives and tolerances are individually different. No view can be taken on faith. Those that appear solid must be verified by market action. Only a novice will buy because an anonymous person on some forum said to; or sell something because a co-worker sold. Only a person with a proven track record deserves your serious attention – providing you realize the differences in your circumstances and know how to incorporate them in your trading decisions. Anyone without a proven record is to be taken with extreme caution until he proves himself through actions. Words are cheap – a track record is the only proof of a trader's skill and prudence.

Another aspect of the third poem applicable to trading is reasonable target setting and position sizing. A trader whose expectations are based on his desires and not rooted in reality tends to overextend himself. His trading position may exceed his risk tolerance, being too large for his account size. His holding time may exceed what is reasonable in an attempt to maximize his profits beyond realistic returns. Just as a Taoist tempers his desires and expectations according to the realities of his life, an astute trader constantly asks himself whether his profit expectations stem from his desires or are confirmed by the observable market actions – realistically aimed at ***"Making full his belly."*** When deciding on his position size, he evaluates the risk and weighs whether he can afford the loss caused by an adverse market movement. He does not allow himself to be blinded by the lure of riches and overextend his position beyond what is tolerable from the point of view of risk. In the same way a trader keeps manageable the number of positions open simultaneously. No matter how many lucrative opportunities are out there, he knows how many positions he is able to monitor, so he won't exceed his abilities and lose focus in a vain attempt to consume everything in sight.

To establish your measuring stick for realistic trade expectations, envision your ideal trade – a realistic one, not the dreamt up one. Calculate what kind of position size will keep you comfortable with risk; envision the ideal development of the trade that takes you into profits that make you happy while remain realistically achievable by the market. Use such a vision to verify your expectation against it; remind yourself of discipline if you catch yourself dreaming of bigger profits and adjusting your trade parameters to those dreams without verifying them with market signals.

A Taoist Trader knows his natural limitations and respects them. He doesn't trade stocks that move too fast for him to manage; he avoids markets that are more volatile than he can stomach. He stays away from the trading vehicles he doesn't know well enough. He doesn't trade setups he doesn't understand.

Just as a Taoist, an experienced trader isn't seduced by the promises of the "cunning ones" – not when it comes to what actions he should undertake, nor when he is promised a "sure thing". He knows there is no certainty in the market and no one knows the future. Promise of a predetermined outcome tells him that he deals with dishonest or ignorant persons.

The importance of the last part of the poem is impossible to overestimate. Let's re-read it before going into trading application:

*"**Action without deeds**" means to ingrain Taoist principles into one's mindset to such degree that they become an integral part of one's character, automatically resulting in correct behavior. The Taoist reacts to situations as they present themselves. He does not try to predict the future, understanding that anything can happen. Such an approach rids him of worries about his predictions coming true. His peace of mind stems from knowing he reacted to events according to sound, robust Taoist principles.*

A trader strives to incorporate the right trading philosophy in his blood. When achieved, his actions become a manifestation of his mindset. He acts automatically, without much deliberation. When a recognizable situation appears, he doesn't need repetitive analysis – he simply executes a familiar course of action, pre-canned response to a familiar situation. He has a set of standard situations (trading setups) and a set of corresponding actions to each turn of events. Trading is not about predicting to him – it's about right reactions. Accumulating more and more familiar situations with responses prepared in advance is his skill-honing process. A Taoist Trader has a set of routines – standard models of behavior designed for variety of situations. In later chapter we will go over this concept in greater details and present such set of routines.

Such an approach frees a trader from the worries about his predictions being right – he does not predict anything. By its very nature, this approach also allows him to leave ego aside – if there is no prediction involved, there won't be a right or wrong side when events unfold, thus no reason for ego to come into the picture. This alone constitutes an enormous step forward in forming the correct psychological state necessary for successful trading.

A Taoist Trader also redefines what a "good" and "bad" trade is. Since anything can happen on any given trade (the market is an uncertain environment), the outcome of trade can not serve as sole measurement of the quality of trading decision. A good trade for him now is the one where he followed his sound and proven trading system, and a bad trade is the one where he broke his trading rules – regardless of outcome. He knows that making good trades (those that match his trading system) will reward him statistically, even if a particular trade results in a loss. He also knows that breaking the rules of his system will result in losses over a long run – even if a particular trade brings him a reward. By following his robust approach, he simply allows natural laws to take their course, without trying to outsmart them and finding his peace of mind in knowing that he was true to his principles. He knows that being in tune with the market and faithful to his principles he will be rewarded.

5.
Nature is Unkind

Nature is unkind;
It treats the creations like sacrificial straw-dogs.
The Sage is unkind;
He treats the people like sacrificial straw-dogs.
How the universe is like a bellows!
Empty, yet it gives a supply that never fails;
The more it is worked, the more it brings forth.
By many words is wit exhausted.
Rather, therefore, hold to the core.

Nature is unkind;
It treats the creations like sacrificial straw-dogs.
The Sage is unkind;
He treats the people like sacrificial straw-dogs.

One of the base principles of Taoism acknowledges that Nature is harsh and not an environment mindful of people's wishes, nor caring to grant them. Attempts to change what can't be changed lead to nothing but frustration and a senseless waste of one's energy. Taoism accepts that Nature can't be changed and gives an individual the tools necessary to coexist with the laws of Nature and find the means of survival and contentment. It is possible for an individual to successfully navigate the way to clarity and be in tune with Nature. This starts by accepting Nature's way as a given – such acceptance is the first step to contentment. Unrealistic expectations will inevitably lead to constant disappointment and make survival all but impossible. Taoists understand that Nature does not take sides, does not punish and does not reward. There are merely consequences of one's actions ruthlessly dished out without partiality.

Taoism states clearly that we are part of Nature and not above it. Our main distinction from animals is free will and ability to analyze our surroundings in a more sophisticated fashion. Together with free will comes a metal disease – pride. Our free will gives us a choice between acceptance or denial or our being a part of nature. If pride pushes us into denial, our chances of survival become less than those of animals, who, in their robust simplicity, live by simple rules of survival; their conduct is not marred by confusion.

The constant flow of confusing messages from social sources obscures reality and encourages us to follow values other than those that serve out best interests.

Oftentimes we are taught complacency without regard to the battle around us. Being complacent and non-confrontational may serve us badly in professional life, in street life and in many decisions we make on daily basis. It's our responsibility to recognize reality for what it is, to sort out the messages sent by society and to manage the consequences of our actions. The slogan "Every man is responsible for his own actions" is inscribed above the entrance of traditional Taoist Temples. Such responsibility includes the necessity to defend ourselves against outside dangers and to protect our health. Practicing a healthy way of life allows us to prevent many problems. Prevention is the application of the Taoist principle of dealing with problems at early stages when it's easier to manage rather than letting it grow.

Equally confusing and damaging can be the siren message of a strong work ethic. While it is instrumental to maintaining a work discipline, this message is often taken to an extreme, turning one's life into endless work. Earning a livelihood and being productive must be done with an appropriate commitment of time and energy; it should not consume an individual's whole life.

A Taoist, using nature as a model, treats society as a whole with the same impartiality. He does not accept the false principle of universal love. His caring is reserved for his "cocoon" – a small group of people close to him.

How the universe is like a bellows!
Empty, yet it gives a supply that never fails;
The more it is worked, the more it brings forth.

*Comparing Tao to a bellows symbolizes the constant reversion between expansion and contraction (Yin and Yang). This cycle is infinite, thus it **"gives a supply that never fails"**. Natural cycles have no preference or partiality – winter is not better than summer, there is no preference to day over night; Nature does not give a better chance to the predator or the prey. By tuning himself to these cycles, a Taoist stands to receive benefits of the natural energy flow (**"the more it is worked, the more it brings forth"**).*

By many words is wit exhausted.
Rather, therefore, hold to the core.

Endless attempts to figure out Nature's manifestations are fruitless. Much overcomplicated thinking obfuscates the simplicity and clarity of the real world. Knowledge must be useful and practical.

Taoism makes a distinction between a true sage and a social sage. True sages speak simple and robust truths. Their message is one of common sense and survival. Social sages blur reality through unnecessarily complex and confusing messages that enables them, and the society they represent, to manipulate people. Their message is one of serving vague higher purposes and self-sacrifice. Therefore, a Taoist "hold to the core," uses nature as his model and adapts his way to Nature and its source, the Tao.

Nature is unkind;
It treats the creations like sacrificial straw-dogs.
The Sage is unkind;
He treats the people like sacrificial straw-dogs.

IN total congruence with Taoism's principle, the market is not a friendly caring environment trying to make you profitable; nor is it forgiving or in any way mindful of you. In fact, it's totally indifferent to you and has no idea you exist – unless you do something to stand out. Being generally not aware of you personally, it doesn't go after you personally either. If sometimes it feels like that, the reason is different. The market works in a way that punishes the majority; thus when you take the majority side instead of the smart money side, the market works against you. If you take certain action and the market immediately reacts as if it watched you and moved to punish you – this is a definite sign that you are making some very common mistake. Such an occurrence and perception is widespread among beginning traders.

To preserve one's emotional balance it's important to realize that the market, just like Nature, is neither kind nor hostile. It is impartial and unbiased; it takes no sides; it has no favorites. If you act correctly, you will be rewarded by profits; if you act incorrectly, you will be ruthlessly punished by losses. Neither is an intended action by the market toward you – it's simply the consequences of your own actions and of the way you structure your interaction with the market.

Having expectations of the market as a friendly environment structured for your benefit will lead to endless frustration. Hoping that the market will care about your needs and desires will lead to endless losses. In the same way that a Taoist regards Nature as a model of pure undistorted reality, a Taoist Trader accepts the harsh cold reality of the market and is ready to face it.

As neither a caring environment, nor one personally hostile toward you, the market can be likened to an ocean. If you learn to read the currents correctly and have the skills, courage and discipline to swim with them, you will reach your destination. Being aligned with the market's energy is your goal. In order to achieve this goal you need to understand the flow of this energy and learn to be a part of it. If, however, you misread the current's direction, don't have the swimming skills or discipline to follow your own understanding, you will drown. Just as a human being is a part of the nature and is not above it; just as an experienced swimmer must become a part of the ocean's currents – an astute trader must become a part of the market in order to be in tune with it.

You can trace this analogy through many levels of market functions. Just as in Nature, in the market the strong prey on the weak. Just as in Nature, there is no mercy toward the losing side of the trade – those caught on the wrong side will have to face their losses, and those on the right side of the trade will not relent.

As humans we have free will, the capacity to pause and choose our response. This will help a Taoist Trader to differentiate himself from the crowd that responds emotionally and instinctively. It is here the key difference will be found – the ability to become a detached observer whose actions are not impacted by his emotions. Instead of impulsive reaction, we elect the way we respond in accordance with our training. At the same time, it's imperative to understand that we are not above the market; we are a part of it. Sometimes even the most powerful market participants forget this and become a victim of their own actions; as they try to push the market in a certain direction and manipulate other traders' perception, they get caught into the trap of their own making. The ebb and flow of the market is a record of the psychology and emotions of the participants and a direct outcome of their decision-making. Being some of participants makes us a part of the market. Its rules and patterns must govern our action; we do not have power to impose our wishes and needs on it. Nor can we hope that we somehow possess the exclusivity that will protect us if our behavior is not aligned with market currents. Attempt to position ourselves above the market would be dictated by pride and ego; such positioning would remove all ties to reality. The right way of thinking and acting is usually simple and robust; it's not overcomplicated and convoluted. It's also ego-free as ego intrusion is what usually distorts our thinking process and removing our conclusions farther and farther from reality.

A wise trader is sensitive to information about the market; he makes an effort to distinguish sincere and truthful information from the messages created with agendas in mind. He knows that no one is supposed to work for his benefit; he is ultimately responsible for his action. Soothing appeal to relax and let the market work for him ("In the long run market always goes up") is a false message; it's not designed to benefit him. "Don't try to time the market", "Loss is not a loss while it's on paper", "Contribute every month to your portfolio and diversify it" are all examples of such harmful messages. An astute trader understands that "market going up in the long run" is a an argument that doesn't hold the water when inflation and index rebalancing are factored in; timing the market is exactly what successful traders do; and paper loss can and will kill trading accounts in a very real way.

Practicing the Taoist principle of prevention, a trader must deal with a problem while it's small. Thus, applying strict stop loss, he prevents the loss from growing and becoming real danger to his trading account. In a similar fashion, seeing that his trading approach ceased working, he will make all efforts to adapt as early as possible, preventing problem from growing.

Continuing analogies, let's touch on the false work ethic. It's one idea that makes a confused trader feel that he is not earning his keep when not trading. Thus, he may feel obliged to participate in action all the time – regardless of whether compelling opportunities are presented. Breaking this notion, a Taoist Trader will stay on the sideline as long as needed, until he obtains a signal from the market.

How the universe is like a bellows!
Empty, yet it gives a supply that never fails;
The more it is worked, the more it brings forth.

Just as bellows provide constant flow of air through expansion and contraction, the market movements do the same. And, just as Nature has no preference to one side over another, the market does not differentiate between up and down, not labeling them as good or bad. A wise trader stays in tune with market rules, equally accepting both directions, expecting them to change and being ready to trade any side. Being in tune with market rhythm, feeling its natural cycle of inhalation and exhalation, a Taoist Trader makes himself available to a constant flow of opportunities and stands to benefit from them. It's very important for a trader to stop giving preference to one side over another; to upward-bound market over downward; to bullish phases over bearish. Being natural parts of the market cycle, they are there for a reason; they are inalienable parts of energy flow and can be used by an impartial and undifferentiating trader.

By many words is wit exhausted.
Rather, therefore, hold to the core.

A wise trader does not delve into endless discussions of vague and overcomplicated matters with no immediate practical implications. He knows that engaging in such activity can cause confusion and incorrect action. Discussion with no practical benefit is of no interest to him. Practical matters promising pragmatic solutions will usually root in realistic, simple and robust matters. He will also pay attention to messages disseminated by market commentators so he can differentiate signal from noise. He will make an effort to distinguish the real sage from the "social" one – one who works for the benefit of certain groups or for himself, without bringing any value to his followers or even hurting their interests. Real sage's advice is practical and verifiable; his message can be applied in practice and the outcome can be observed. This outcome must positive for his followers on a regular basis. If, however, an advice regularly leads to a negative outcome, yet the sage continues insisting on "staying the course", denies errors, hides his record or blames the outcome on the followers, he is to be dismissed as a false guru.

7.
Living For Others

The universe is everlasting.
The reason the universe is everlasting
Is that it does not live for Self.
Therefore it can long endure.
Therefore the Sage puts himself last,
And finds himself in the foremost place;
Regards his body as accidental,
And his body is thereby preserved.
Is it not because he does not live for Self
That his Self is realized?

This chapter and its very title are somewhat deceptive. On the surface, it reads like the traditional, societal, "virtue" of sacrificing oneself for others, which contradicts one of the cornerstone Taoist principles of pursuing natural self-interest. In reality, a more accurate translation would be "Living Among Others." This poem is rather a warning to comprehend the systems surrounding us and to evaluate our place within them. It's also deceptively simple-looking while in reality it offers insight into fairly complex matters.

The most important system impacting our well-being is society. Taoism recognizes it as a social food chain in which the individual is an insignificant participant. Thus, ***Living for Others*** *is a reminder that we must adopt a humble, defensive posture in order to survive. It alerts us that in order to live a content life we need to make ourselves compliant to larger forces, align ourselves with natural laws (****the Sage puts himself last And finds himself in the foremost place****).*

The poem concludes with a rhetorical question whether by not living for "Self," don't we become more "realized"?

This concept of "not living for Self" in order to "realize Self" says that placing the Self "last" is necessary in order to see and understand the system much larger than any single individual. Those are systems with which we need to co-exist, understand our place within them, and then navigate among their powerful forces. We are subservient to these forces and any attempt to try to be "first" (place oneself above them) is a doomed pursuit. The Taoist uses the Tao Te Ching's principles to tap the power of these forces while avoiding their wrath.

Chuang Tzu, a later Taoist philosopher, urges us to "unite ***all things and become impartial.****" He wrote that the systems around us are complex structures without biases. The individual components may have differences, but one is not favored over the other – all of them are necessary* *for the system's functionality. A car's designer is not partial to an engine, steering wheel or tires – each component is included to make the vehicle a functioning whole. Chuang Tzu illustrates this point with another pair of natural and social examples:* ***"The four seasons are different in temperature not by the individual decisions of heavens; thus it is possible to have a complete year. The officials of the five departments have different duties conferred impartially by the ruler; thus it is possible to have a unified nation."***

The ability to recognize the Oneness around us requires viewing all components equally so as to not become focused on a small piece of the bigger picture and not to become partial to any of them. Because people ***"usually look at things from their respective points of view, and miss the truth,"*** *we must try to dispassionately analyze the systems around us. This explains why the poem urges the Taoist to place "Self" last so his emotions do not blind him to reality through ill-advised partiality.*

To stand outside any phenomenon requires setting aside the restricted vision of preconceived notions and the emotional baggage. Achieving this state of detachment is akin to that rare military commander who can maintain composure during the "fog of war," understand the situation, and then act with objective dispassion. Developing holistic vision is necessary to grasp the overall situation; then action must be taken to best deal with the forces affecting the Taoist. Comprehending the systems with which we deal can only be fruitful if we act upon this knowledge. Such action is not defined as an attempt to change the system but instead to coexist within the system/society while living a content life.

Chuang Tzu points out a key aspect when he writes, ***"There is a before and an after in time, and the world is in continual change."*** *Here he expounds on the Principle of Reversion according to which the systems around us are in a state of constant rotation. There are cycles to every phenomenon and nothing is stagnant. The Taoist recognizes that seasons change from summer to winter and back; days follow nights; empires grow and then decline. The Sage will be better at tolerating bad times by acknowledging that,* ***"Fortune and misfortune follow one another; there is some good in what at first displeases."*** *Basically, Chuang Tzu advises us to not get overly happy when times are good and not become too despondent when times are tough.*

Since rotation is a sign of all healthy systems, we should avoid situations that are stagnant: still water becomes foul, stale relationships become tired, non-responsive companies become broke, and stagnant minds become confused.

The universe is everlasting.
The reason the universe is everlasting
Is that it does not live for Self.
Therefore it can long endure.

AN individual trader striving to comprehend his place in the market must realize the enormous imbalance between market forces and his powers. It is absolutely necessary to avoid attempts to outsmart and out-stubborn the market. Humility in understanding his place and role in the market goes a long way in a trader's survival. The old adage "the market is always right" addresses just this concept. Let's think of the dangers of "putting Self first". It is when a trader decides that he is smarter than the market that he starts averaging down on his losing position instead of cutting his loss; tries to hold onto that position, and rationalizes his action by thinking that he "won't let them fool him." Such thinking is clearly dictated by ego. Market forces usually take the price much further in the adverse direction than what a trader can endure. Another well-known market adage describes this phenomenon: "The market can stay irrational longer than you can stay solvent."

Therefore the Sage puts himself last,
And finds himself in the foremost place;
Regards his body as accidental,
And his body is thereby preserved.
Is it not because he does not live for Self
That his Self is realized?

A Taoist Trader understands his place in the "food chain" of the market. He realizes that a small fish does not survive by attacking a large one head on. It survives by understanding the migration and feeding patterns and aligning itself with them in a way that allows it to avoid becoming someone's food while finding its own. It is by studying and understanding the currents around us that we find the way to swim effortlessly. Similarly, learning to spot the prevailing trends and allowing the market to carry his position in the direction of those trends, an astute trader aligns himself with powerful market forces instead of fighting them.

In accordance with Chuang Tzu'steaching, a trader must see the unity of all market elements and remain impartial. It calls for equal perception of both bull and bear phases of the market cycle, without assigning "good" and "bad" labels to any of them. A trader has to realize that each of these phases has its role and the market equally needs both. The market can't go up exclusively just as day can't continue eternally. Night is as natural a part of Nature's cycle as downward movements are in the market. Perceiving both phases as normal parts of the market, a trader becomes capable of utilizing them equally.

Similarly, a trader must remain emotionally detached about any group of market participants. Anger toward more powerful institutions does not serve a trader's interest and can only upset his emotional balance, causing irrational and personally harmful behavior. Influential market participant acting against an individual trader's position is to be perceived as a natural force with which a trader needs to align. Each group has its place in the eternal market flux. It is more influential players that cause those same movements that smaller trader needs in order to make his profit – thus, he needs those powerful players and he must understand how they operate.

Equally, market participants operating in different time frames are all needed for the market to function. There is no better or worse time frame; they are all elements of the same food chain in the market where players operating in higher time frames create more powerful waves for shorter term traders to utilize. Smaller time frame traders, in turn, provide liquidity for the bigger players when the time comes for those to initiate or unwind their position. Disdain of longer term players toward day traders is as meaningless as the opposite; both groups need each other to function smoothly.

Being impartial to any of the elements and forces and remaining humble toward them, a Taoist Trader realizes his place as a natural part of the market environment. Understanding the role of each element provides a healthy foundation for discerning market action. Understanding the eternal cycles, the ebb and flow and constant change of the market, seeing the role each group plays in those changes and understanding how those changes influence each group, allows a trader to foresee the most likely reactions and developments.

This state of mind creates the objectivity and emotional impartiality necessary for a trader to become a detached observer. Clarity of vision not clouded by preconceived notions is necessary for decoding market information. Understanding his role helps a trader stay humble, fluid and dispassionate. The impact of emotions on one's trading decisions can be devastating. Achieving this mindset free of emotional baggage and being in tune with market forces opens a possibility of effortless and stress-free trading. A trader achieving this mindset is capable of easy action and quick smooth decision-making. Just as Chuang Tzu recommends, such trader is able to handle tough times more easily as he is always ready for them: an understanding of the concept of constant change keeps him prepared for the end of easier times.

8.
Water

The best of men is like water;
Water benefits all things
And does not compete with them.
It dwells in (the lowly) places that all disdain –
Wherein it comes near to Tao.
In dwelling, (the Sage) loves the (lowly) earth;
In his heart, he loves what is profound;
In his relations with other, he loves kindness;
In his words, he loves sincerity;
In government, he loves peace;
In business affairs, he loves ability;
In his actions, he loves choosing the right time.
It is because he does not contend
That he is without reproach.

Water is one of the important models provided by Nature. The characteristics of water are one of Taoism's fundamental principles. One of the most significant attributes of the water is how it expresses non-interference – also known as the principle of ***Wu Wei.***

Water provides the model for an individual's ability to navigate peacefully through society. Its characteristics also relate to physical health and psychological well being. Taoism's health-related practices use water as their principle of how energy flows operate.

First, and foremost, water is clear and healthy when it flows smoothly. If it rushes too fast, it's turbulent, or conversely, becomes noxious if stagnant. In Taoist disciplines, the flow of chi (energy) in the body and in the living environment should be corrected in ways to mimic smooth flowing water, free of stagnating blockages and not chaotically rushing about.

Chuang Tzu also describes how the health of the mind emulates water:

When the mind is overworked without stop, it becomes worried, and worry causes exhaustion... Calm represents the nature of water at its best. In that it may serve as our model, for its power is preserved and is not dispersed through agitation.

The best of men is like water;
Water benefits all things
And does not compete with them.

One of water's most significant virtues is that it "does not compete," flowing along its path, calmly flowing around obstacles. Similarly, as a Taoist emulates water, he continues along his path avoiding obstacles and unnecessary conflicts. He does not compete with others by deliberately choosing different goals. Avoiding competition, he is likely to escape adversaries and "benefit all things," because he creates no reason for conflict.

It dwells in (the lowly) places that all disdain –
Wherein it comes near to Tao.

Water naturally moves downward, always seeking the lowest point, flowing around any obstacles. In the same fashion, the Taoist attempts to follow his self-interest, regardless of contrary social values and other people's interests. To "dwell in (the lowly) places that all disdain," means avoiding showing off and attracting unwanted attention by demonstrating one's superiority. By staying under the radar, the Taoist avoids unneeded challenges and saves energy from being wasted on pointless competition. A position of humility is a Taoist's adopted stance – it allows him to avoid triggering his own Ego and others' envy or jealousy. Neither does he strive to disclose philosophical beliefs that are different from those espoused by society. Differences in philosophical outlooks can trigger anger easily; the idea of thinking for oneself and holding personal values different from those of society is anathema to most people.

In dwelling, (the sage) loves the (lowly) earth;
In his heart, he loves what is profound;

Finding one's natural core is the goal of the Sage. He looks to the "profound" principles exhibited in Nature as a model for life, in contrast to the artificial values propagated by the social sages and used by the masses to construct their lives.

In his relations with others, he loves kindness;

The Sage does not treat others unkindly, unnecessarily. Such behavior is a form of needless interference; it calls for reciprocation and creates conflict. The Sage avoids clashes unless necessary to maintain his path.

In Chuang Tzu's words,
There is nothing weaker than water
But nothing is superior to it in overcoming the hard,
for which there is no substitute.

The water's power comes from its flexibility; i.e. – its adaptability. When confronted by an obstacle, water patiently adapts. It may find an alternate route, or slowly wear am obstacle down, or evaporate away. By going around obstacles without contention, it appears weak, yet its persistence accomplishes its goal.

In his words, he loves sincerity;

In a Taoist's view, words are cheap. In evaluating people, he pays attention to whether the words reflect actions. The Sage's actions reflect the principles of which he speaks; discrepancy reveals hypocrisy. A Taoist will regard as hypocrites those whose words differ from their actions.

In government, he loves peace;

For an individual, governing oneself harmoniously is to achieve contentment. Contentment is both purpose and measurement. Actions are constructed to achieve contentment; contentment as envisioned by an individual is a measurement of the sensibility of actions.

In business affairs, he loves ability;

Ability and competence may not sound very "spiritual," but Taoism is a very practical philosophy keeping one's feet firmly on Earth. As such it acknowledges that to survive you must sustain physical needs. Therefore, it is necessary to be productive to earn the money needed for contentment. Just as the Taoist must refine his skills in various disciplines, the same dedication is required in commercial endeavors. Complete commitment to the moment is requisite to executing life's necessities and achieving one's purposes.

In his actions, he loves choosing the right time.

Stated simply, correct action is the right act at the appropriate time. A Taoist chooses a course of action that keeps him on his natural path. He has the discipline to identify when he should expend energy to maintain his path, regardless of irrational desires. Therefore, like calm water, the Taoist's mind is clear, free from the cloudy confusion of turbulent water when choosing "the right time."

It is because he does not contend
That he is without reproach.

As we form our mental model of the world, we must remain mindful of our limitations, be it in physical abilities, in entrepreneurship or in our dealings with the social structure. We need to evaluate realistically our abilities and structure our actions according to evaluation. We pick our battles carefully and do not contend without absolute necessity.

The best of men is like water;
Water benefits all things
And does not compete with them.

JUST as smooth flow facilitates water's health and clarity, steady and smooth trading is the best way to manage risk and guarantee steady profits. Wild swings of one's trading account signify an abnormal amount of risk being taken. Such trading ruins a trader's emotional and mental balance and leads to severe drawdowns. They are emotionally draining and psychologically damaging;

they are also potentially ruinous for the trading account itself as the size of the drawdown can become unsustainable very quickly. A Taoist Trader guards against too much turbulence in his trading and moderates his risk taking in an attempt to prevent severe setbacks.

A trader should apply the same principle to his reading of market movements. It helps him understand whether a movement is in its sustainable stage or is coming to its end, thus enabling him to decide whether to hold his position or start looking for an exit. Smooth steady price movement with stable volume is likely to be sustainable and continue for a while. Parabolic turbulent price movement with exploding volume signals an approaching final stage.– such extreme price/volume action is not sustainable and will lead to a reversal sooner rather than later.

It dwells in (the lowly) places that all disdain –
Wherein it comes near to Tao.

Picking his stocks, a trader avoids the most risky volatile ones – just as a Taoist chooses his path without unnecessary conflicts and competition. A Taoist Trader also avoids those stocks and sectors where there is not enough volatility, remembering that stagnant water turns rotten. Finding the stocks and sectors with healthy, smooth, liquid movement is a trader's purpose.

In dwelling, (the sage) loves the (lowly) earth;
In his heart, he loves what is profound;

A trader with unusually big position to initiate or unwind will avoid attracting unneeded attention. If he shows his intentions, he is likely to encounter a lot of smaller orders undercutting his, trying to take advantage of the information he carelessly revealed, thus hampering his task. If you see unusually big orders shown openly, there is a good chance they are fake – rarely will a skillful player demonstrate his true intentions.

As water tends to gash through the broken dam once it overcomes its resistance, a market often starts a strong movement after breaking through mighty support or resistance. Many breakout or breakdown trading setups are based on this principle. A Taoist Trader uses this observation to place himself in the center of the action when he finds strong resistance or support being tested time and again.

In his relations with others, he loves kindness;

A wise trader does not try to overcome the market's mood or trend. Adaptability is his strongest trait – similarly to water, he finds his strength in what seems to be weakness. He won't push strongly when there is not much activity in the market. He won't try to go against the current trend. He will listen carefully to the market's voice, stay sensitive to changes and adapt to them naturally and effortlessly.

In his words, he loves sincerity;

In picking his information sources, a skillful trader will carefully observe whether a commentator's message is consistent and truthful. Only a verified track record of correct market evaluations proves the commentator's knowledge and skill. Contrarily, and in keeping with Lao Tzu's message, "The bad man is the lesson of the good." a skillful trader will carefully observe if a commentator's message is often a contrary indicator in regards to market action. Clarity, practicality, humility and honesty are necessary traits of someone worthy following. At the same time, even following a tried and true source, a trader must remember that his own objectives might be different. Thus, he stays true to his core and listens to his instincts.

In business affairs, he loves ability;

Choosing his trading approach, position size and holding period, a trader must evaluate his own level of comfort. While challenging himself in order to improve, he does not overextend his abilities and tries to stay content. Too large position can make a trader uncomfortable with the level of the risk he is taking. Psychological discomfort can easily cause suboptimal decisions. Mental balance and contentment are necessary components of a calm and objective decision-making process.

In his actions, he loves choosing the right time.

Timing is one of the most important aspects of correct trading. No matter how correct one's idea of the general market direction, his trade won't be successful unless timed well. A Taoist Trader will always question his timing by checking whether his reason for initiating the trade existed earlier yet hasn't led to a trade being profitable. In other words, if the reason for a certain direction change in the market has been presented for a while yet the direction stays the same – it means a trader's idea lacks the necessary timing signals. Designing his trading system, a skillful trader will pay great attention to a matter of timing. He will test his approach thoroughly making sure that his entry and exit signals occur at optimal moments. When his system is carefully designed and thoroughly tested, a trader's mind is calm and clear. He knows that the odds are on his side and his risk is controlled by pre-determined parameters.

**It is because he does not contend
That he is without reproach.**

A Taoist trader knows himself well. He understands his abilities and limitations. He structures his trading in a way that conforms to his comfort level, risk tolerance, execution abilities and personality traits. He understands that trading is not a "one size fits all" endeavor. There is no single right way to trade. One's right way to trade is a way that matches both the laws of the market and the trader's personality. His trading strategy can be in accordance with market conditions, yet unfit for a particular trader's risk profile or too slow for him. It may require bigger capital than he possesses or lead to longer holding times than his objectives demand. By incorporating both, market conditions and his personal requirements in his trading strategy a trader finds the optimal spot – a strategy that leads to a desired result.

9.
The Danger of Overweening Success

Stretch (a bow) to the very full,
And you will wish you had stopped in time.
Temper a (sword-edge) to its very sharpest,
And the edge will not last long.
When gold and jade fill your hall,
You will not be able to keep them safe.
To be proud with wealth and honor
Is to sow the seeds of one's own downfall.
Retire when your work is done,
Such is Heaven's way.

Stretch (a bow) to the very full,
And you will wish you had stopped in time.

*In archery, it's necessary to stop drawing the bowstring in time to avoid breaking the bow. This analogy illustrates one of the cornerstone tenets of Taoism: every phenomenon has finite limits which should not be exceeded. Just as the bow is limited by its maximum draw length, so too are humans limited physically and intellectually, even though our desires may push us beyond our capacities. Pushing too far creates an imbalance, which can break the mind and body; and **"you will wish that you had stopped in time."***

Temper a (sword edge) to its very sharpest,
And the edge will not last long.

When a sword is honed to its absolute sharpest, the edge of the blade becomes either too brittle or so flexible that it easily bends, rendering the weapon unusable. Therefore, optimal functionality comes from a blade sharpened to the level appropriate for the natural state of its steel and for the task. This Taoist metaphor warns against pursuing idealized standards that can become counter-productive. Idealizations should not be part of life's goals, and instead, be limited to our individual capabilities and natural limitations. The Yin/Yang symbol that has dots of opposite colors symbolizes the impossibility of perfect white or perfect black-thus perfection is impossibility.

Society often pushes us to exceed our natural limits by fostering unhealthy competition in pursuit of formulas for success. Some competition, like conflict, is inevitable in life, but a Taoist should try to only "compete" with himself, and use comparisons with others as a tool for learning, for evaluating his weaknesses and improving his performance, because there will always be someone smarter, faster, stronger, better.

When gold and jade fill your hall,
You will not be able to keep them safe.

Acquiring excessive material possessions is a misguided pursuit of things that can't be taken with us at death. Further, keeping them ***"safe"*** *is not a sure bet either. Accumulating too much of material possessions makes us targets of envy and jealousy. Is not the recent financial bubble such evidence?*

To be proud with wealth and honor
Is to sow the seeds of one's own downfall.

Pride cometh before the fall. Overwhelming success breeds overconfidence and arrogance and triggers the beginning of the downfall. The overconfident individual begins to overlook critical details in decision-making and tends to start attributing his success to his personal traits instead of his well thought through actions. This leads to loose discipline reinforced by a false feeling of invincibility.

Another aspect of a loss is the "downfall" of one's spirit. When material attachments run too deep, an individual risks his or her daily contentment. If one's measure of contentment is dependent on possessions, then their loss places contentment in jeopardy.

Taoists understand that pride over one's material success is inappropriate because aside from talent and discipline, uncontrollable chance plays a significant role in material success. You can make your own luck to an extent, but good fortune is also a consequence of unknown factors.

Retire when your work is done,
Such is Heaven's way.

It is not uncommon to see those who could comfortably retire continue to work. It may be caused by fear of losing material comfort, or by not knowing what to do with oneself with all of the extra spare time; it could be an outcome of conditioning by society that emphasizes being a hard worker as an honor, or, perhaps, work is what truly makes us happy.

According to Lao Tzu, when things are good enough, we should "retire" or stop. Like over-sharpening a sword, pushing too far can ruin the result. Taoist philosophy warns that the hardest thing to do is to stop "when your work is done." It takes a deep understanding one's limitations to recognize the moment when the best result is achieved.

Stretch (a bow) to the very full,
And you will wish you had stopped in time.
Temper a (sword edge) to its very sharpest,
And the edge will not last long.

MOST traders have encountered phenomena of an abrupt end to a successful streak. After a long period of winning, the moment comes when a trader suddenly stops doing those things that made him successful. It's not an accident that this often occurs after a strong winning streak. In the same way as overstretching the bow or over-sharpening the sword breaks it or renders it useless, a trader's mind loses its sharpness and his discipline becomes loose if a trader allows success to go to his head. He tends to become careless and overconfident. Worse yet, his ego springs into action whispering in his ear that he is invincible. All his discipline and rules go out the window, and a string of devastating losses ensues. A Taoist Trader understands this danger and stays sensitive to subtle changes. He remembers that all phenomena pushed to an extreme tend to reverse and turn into their opposites. He strives to sense the moment when his good fortune changes in order to become more careful, reinforce his discipline and renew his commitment to humility.

In a similar fashion, great, strong trends in the market tend to reverse after reaching their apogee. An astute trader will become more and more reserved in his trend-following trades as he sees overwhelming confidence in trend continuation among his peers and media types. As the first signs of changes in the trading environment appear against the background of mass confidence in the trend, he will start looking for trend reversal trades. At a minimum, he will pull back from pushing strongly in the previously established direction to preserve himself from devastating losses in case of sudden change in market direction. He also understands the danger of slow subtle changes that do not raise alarm in most traders. Psychological inertia makes them dismiss those changes as temporary setbacks of no importance. As a result they will expect a bounce back and resumption of a previous trend. Meanwhile, a trend reversal becomes a very unforgiving environment that, unlike trend continuation, does not allow easy recovery from errors. If the changes in trend come in a slow gradual fashion, a wise trader will be ready for that – decreased activity will save him from such inertia and complacency.

When gold and jade fill your hall,
You will not be able to keep them safe.

Following sound Taoist advice of avoiding material attachments, a wise trader will avoid focusing too much on his profits and losses. He understands that the subject of his job as a trader is reading the market correctly and keeping strict discipline. Monetary success will come naturally as a reward for a job well done. Focusing on the reward instead of the job at hand is a serious distraction. Concentrating on the monetary side takes a trader's focus off of market developments, making him likely to miss important signals. It also introduces emotions that distort his perceptions and obfuscate objectivity.

Retire when your work is done,
Such is Heaven's way.

One of the hardest things to do as a trader is to retreat from the action and stay on the sideline. When the risk becomes intolerable; when the trend shows signs of exhaustion (in a typical Taoist paradox it is usually the moment when the trend seems to be the most powerful and unstoppable); when a trader's success reaches its apogee (again, the warning sign of a peak being reached) – it means that the "**work is done**" and it's time to retreat, re-group and re-evaluate.

10.
Embracing the One

In embracing the One with your soul,
Can you never forsake the Tao?
In controlling your vital force to achieve gentleness,
Can you become like the new-born child?
In cleansing and purifying your Mystic vision,
Can you strive after perfection?
In loving the people and governing the kingdom,
Can you rule without interference?
In opening and shutting the Gate of Heaven,
Can you play the part of the Female?
In comprehending all knowledge,
Can you renounce the mind?
To give birth, to nourish,
To give birth without taking possession,
To act without appropriation,
To be chief among men without managing them -
This is the Mystic Virtue.

This poem summarizes many of the Taoist principles in a series of questions that confront the individual's commitment to the Taoist teachings. Practical disciplined implementation is significantly more difficult than theoretical studies. These are just words on paper; can you manifest them in your actions?

In embracing the One with your soul,
Can you never forsake the Tao?

The concept of all phenomena being manifestations of "one" is a cornerstone of Taoism. It can be difficult to constantly view the events and developments through this prism. This stanza asks whether the reader can fully commit to such discipline. This commitment is an eternal one, so you "can never forsake the Tao."

In controlling your vital force to achieve gentleness,
Can you become like the new-born child?

Achieving "gentleness" refers to a state of Wu Wei – non- interference. A Taoist has to allow his original nature – the healthy natural instincts, to govern his life, while resisting society's effort to push artificial values on him. The "new-born child," an oft repeated reference in the Tao Te Ching, represents the state of mind in which we are uncorrupted by unnatural values. The child's instincts are pure, with responses to external stimuli completely natural. The flexibility of a newborn allows him to persevere under straining circumstances, while the rigidity of older people makes them vulnerable.

In cleansing and purifying your Mystic vision,
Can you strive after perfection?

"Perfection" is contentment in daily life. "Mystic Vision" refers to the way we absorb information. "Cleansing and purifying" refers to the mental exercises helping us preserve clarity and avoid confusion. We gather information, analyze our options and choose a course of action. Philosophical principles provide guidelines, standards against which we measure alternatives. The Taoist meditative disciplines, at their most basic level, are designed to quiet the mind, allowing it to rest, thus reducing the noise of outside influences which cloud our thinking. They also reduce the mental stress of daily life that contributes to sub-optimal decision-making.

Sometimes complicated, seemingly intractable problems find no resolution despite endless worrying and insistent search. Finally, at some point, when walking away from a problem or sitting quietly, a sudden burst of enlightenment breaks the mental blockage and the solution becomes obvious. This quiet moment which enabled clear thinking is exactly the condition Taoists create during meditation.

In loving the people and governing the kingdom,
Can you rule without interference?

This stanza would read more accurate by replacing the word "loving" with "accepting." Just as a mother accepts her child, no matter its strength or illnesses, so too, a Taoist must accept people around him for what they are and not interfere with their natural constitutions.

In opening and shutting the Gate of Heaven,
Can you play the part of the Female?

The "Gate of Heaven" is the mind. The mind must be willing to accept the concepts and to dedicate the effort needed to implement them. The "Female" in this stanza is a reference to the yin principle, which represents flexibility. The information around us is available for the taking – however to absorb it and use it in a constructive way the individual must free himself from the artificial beliefs. Given the persistence and omnipresence of the external "programming," it takes a lot of courage to be flexible enough to accept reality.

In comprehending all knowledge,
Can you renounce the mind?

In Taoist philosophy, there are two types of knowledge: useable knowledge that contributes to the achievement of a goal (daily contentment), and knowledge that does not. The only knowledge worth pursuing is the knowledge that serves the purpose. Our ability to adapt to changes in an environment is a double-edged sword. Our mind sometimes accepts external values without skepticism. These values often conflict with our core nature and represent dysfunctional knowledge. However, by using Taoist principles, we can accurately evaluate which knowledge is worth keeping and which should be discarded.

To give birth, to nourish,
To give birth without taking possession,
To act without appropriation,

Material possessions should be pursued sufficiently to support life. "Taking possession" implies trying to keep something with force, implying intrusion, which contravenes Lao Tzu's principle of non-interference – Wu Wei.

To be chief among men without managing them -
This is the Mystic Virtue.

The Sage realizes there are few people with the necessary willpower to truly follow the Taoist teachings; most are comfortable to remain part of the crowd. Therefore, the Sage does not try to convert the masses, but simply focuses his efforts on those few who cross his path. In a similar sense, the good leader ideally practices laissez-faire in managing society, trying to allow each citizen's nature to be realized. For an individual, personal refinement is a continuous process that takes patience and requires discipline. Taoists strive to effectively use the Taoist principles, focus the mind; control the body; realize his limitations; know when to act and when not to act; camouflage, and guard against "desires of the mind." Discipline enables the Taoist to avoid confusion that distracts from the present moment.

In embracing the One with your soul,
Can you never forsake the Tao?

FOR a trader it is important to view the market as constant uninterrupted flow of interconnected events where nothing exists in vacuum and everything influences everything. All the elements forming the market and all the information influencing the behavior of the participants combines into a united "big picture." To navigate his way through the market, a trader needs constantly to maintain the big picture. Each trend in a time frame chosen by a trader exists within a bigger trend in a larger time frame – and it is beneficial to make sure those are aligned. Each company belongs to a certain sector or industry; sectors compile the market as a whole and define its "mood" as well as depend on it – and a trader needs to evaluate these mutual influences. Each source of information presents certain opinions, which may or may not be objective – it's crucial to see through the possible biases. Finally, the market itself is but a slice of the societal structure and exists in an interaction and interdependence with economics and politics. Focusing on too narrow a slice of the market, too limited a time-frame, or a biased source of information, leads to an incomplete and distorted view of the market, and thus an erroneous course of action.

In controlling your vital force to achieve gentleness,
Can you become like the new-born child?

For a trader, the "new-born child"-like state of mind can manifest itself in two valuable skills. One is flexibility in decision-making, absence of directional bias or rigid opinion on a certain position. Being locked in such biases and opinions renders a trader unable to see his error, triggers his ego, and leads to a stubborn attempt to overpower market forces. This is not a trivial state of mind – we are taught that a strong confident individual must have his opinions and stand by them. Changing our views on a dime is considered a sign of weakness, lack of confidence or absence of beliefs. An individual conforming to such external views will look "normal" to society, and a trader – to those around him; however, he will pay a high price for this acceptance by losing his ability to stay in tune with the market and remain flexible enough to respond to the changes.

Another skill is the ability to listen to one's natural intuition. A Taoist Trader knows its value and possesses the ability to clear his mind of external noise, allowing his natural instincts to respond to a situation and guide him through a trade. If a trader's mind is unpolluted by all the propaganda and financial "advice" imposed by the plethora of gurus, he is free to listen to the only speaker who knows the ultimate truth – the market itself. The voice of intuition is a quiet one. A trader needs to be in a calm unhurried state of mind to hear it.

In cleansing and purifying your Mystic vision,
Can you strive after perfection?

A trader must have his general trading philosophy worked out. Such a philosophy outlines his understanding of how the market works, what major forces determine its direction, how they interact between themselves and what footprints they leave in a process for a trader to read. Having guidelines, a trader can measure the information he receives from the market action against it. This is a Taoist Trader's main weapon against confusion; structured and clearly defined approaches allow him to preserve clarity of mind and mental balance. This also serves as a necessary starting point for intuition to spring into action. When a trader with a robust clear understanding of the market gathers the necessary information as an unemotional detached observer and quiets his mind allowing it to process the information, the decision-making process becomes quick and effortless. For a side observer it would almost seem as if decisions come to a trader from some outside source, in the form of a solution given by someone else. In reality, it's a natural outcome of the correct approach aligned with natural law and having a solid, sound system. Not unlike a skilled fighter who moves with lightening speed and seemingly pre-empts all the moves of the opponent before they are even made, a skillful trader is able to act rapidly and effortlessly thanks to preparation, extensive practice and a well thought out approach.

In loving the people and governing the kingdom,
Can you rule without interference?

As a Taoist accepts people around him for what they are, a wise trader accepts all market participants and their actions without passing judgment on them, without assigning blame or evaluating their actions emotionally. Any market participant acting against a Taoist Trader's position does not get labeled as an enemy and does not become the subject of anger. Only an unbalanced confused trader experiences and expresses anger toward a seller who suppresses his long position or a buyer who supports the price against his short. Such emotional perception clouds judgment and prevents a trader from calculated cold-blooded action. Instead, any adverse market player, commentator or event must be taken with no emotional involvement.

In opening and shutting the Gate of Heaven,
Can you play the part of the Female?

An astute trader preserves a flexible mind. He maintains an ability to change course as he absorbs new information. Rigidity in a quickly changing fluid environment is a huge impediment. A trader must remain impartial to opinions imposed on him by market commentators and remain free to form his course of actions without external intrusion – reviewing and changing his course as situation dictates.

In comprehending all knowledge,
Can you renounce the mind?

The amount of information surrounding the markets is mind-boggling. Some of it is useful in the process of decision-making and some serves no useful purpose at all. A trader carefully observes which information helps him navigate the markets and which wastes his time and adds to confusion. Practical usefulness measured by actual performance is a trader's criterion to evaluate which sources should be taken into account and which should be dismissed. A trader must avoid paralysis caused by endless and contradictive information flows.

To give birth, to nourish,
To give birth without taking possession,
To act without appropriation,

Coming up with trading ideas, we must remain objective and uninvolved emotionally. It's easy to "**appropriate**" the idea, to become emotionally attached to it and lose the ability to evaluate it objectively. Criticism by skeptics can make a trader act defensively and fall in love with his idea even more as his ego becomes involved and needs to be protected. "**Giving birth without taking possession**" means remaining emotionally distant and dispassionate. Impartiality helps evaluate the idea on its own merits, without perceiving it as something to cherish and defend.

To be chief among men without managing them -
This is the Mystic Virtue.

Most traders do not operate in vacuum. They interact with others in different forms, be it a trading room, forum or blog. It's important to avoid being impacted by the opinions of others, taking them instead as information to analyze critically. Equally, expressing his own opinions, a trader should not try to convince his counterparts, letting them evaluate his words without heated argument. Those are a waste of time and serve no useful purpose. Differences in opinions are a natural sign of healthy exchange, and in fact, are necessary for market function. Express your thoughts, listen to others, analyze whether they coalesce into a better understanding of the events, decide whether to include this information in your outlook or dismiss it – and let others do the same.

11.
The Utility of Not-Being

Thirty spokes unite around the nave;
From their not-being (loss of their individuality)
Arises the utility of the wheel.
Mold clay into a vessel;
From its not-being (in the vessel's hollow)
Arises the utility of the vessel.
Cut out doors and windows in the house (-wall),
From their not-being (empty space) arises the utility of the house.
Therefore by the existence of things we profit.
And by the non-existence of things we are served.

Lao Tzu's first stanza describes the mechanism for communication between cosmic energy and the individual:

Thirty spokes unite around the nave;
From their not-being (loss of their individuality)
Arises the utility of the wheel.

The spokes represent individuals with their own unique thoughts and motivations. The nave (the wheel's hub) represents the social structure which binds the individual to his community. The combination of the spokes and nave give utility (functionality) to the wheel (society). Just as the wheel works flawlessly when the spokes are precisely similar, society works the smoothest when the difference between individuals is minimized. Aligning themselves too closely with the societal nave, the individual risks the loss of individuality, and may in essence become a tool of society at the loss of self.

However, free will gives us the opportunity to align ourselves with the nave of the universe and its eternal principles, instead of the nave of society. Consciously choosing from which one we take our principles is one of life's most important decisions.

Chuang Tzu's essay, The Tao of God and the Tao of Man, addresses the critical choice of where one looks for guiding principles:

The Tao of God is fundamental: the Tao of man is accidental.
The distance which separates them is great.
Let us all take heed thereto!

The Tao of Man is reflected in temporary moral codes which vary from society to society and one time period to another. Their transience is a result of not being principles but, instead, man-made creations – often in conflict with the principles of Nature. By tuning oneself to the frequency of temporary social structures, one foregoes the benefits of Universal Oneness, with potentially negative implications for one's quest for a content life.

The Taoist Principles of Duality and Reversion teach that all phenomena are composed of opposites working together in an ever-rotating harmony. Daylight and darkness compose a complete day and the four seasons complete a year. According to the Tao Te Ching, understanding comes when seeing both sides of the coin. While the utility of being, having a physical body, is relatively self-evident – the utility of non-existence, or not-being, is less obvious.

Mold clay into a vessel;
From its not-being (in the vessel's hollow)
Arises the utility of the vessel.

Cut out doors and windows in the house (-wall),
From their not-being (empty space) arises the utility of the house.

These examples of a vessel's empty space and those created in a dwelling's walls demonstrate how something seemingly invisible or non-existent can be useful. The empty space of a vessel allows it to hold liquids. The empty spaces cut into walls serve as doors and windows, and the empty space formed by the walls provides shelter and a place to live.

Chuang Tzu in his essay, The Usefulness of Not-Being, writes:

All sentient life depends on the breath.
When the breath is disturbed, it is not the fault of nature.
Nature keeps it open day and night without cease, but man continuously blocks it up.

The "breath" here is a metaphor for "chi," the universal energy of which all living things is composed. It is the central to Taoism's holistic theory of reality. It is important that the "breath" not be blocked up so that chi could freely flow for a healthy body. We disturb our breath and "continuously block it up" when we are distracted by the false values and ideals. In Taoist theory, the noise of social chatter can affect whether we become harmonized with the energy of the Universe or "blocked up" to the point of eventual spiritual dissolution.

Therefore by the existence of things we profit.
And by the non-existence of things we are served.

The poem ends with a metaphor for the duality of our existence. We "profit" by attending to the physical needs of life while directing appropriate effort to the refinement of the soul. "We are served" by "not being" a tool of society. This does not mean escaping our community duties. Instead, spiritual development requires interaction with the world, while consciously differentiating between what is good for society and what is good for the individual, and then acting accordingly.

Thirty spokes unite around the nave;
From their not-being (loss of their individuality)
Arises the utility of the wheel.

THE spokes-and-wheel stanza has a few immediately obvious trading applications. First is one we touched on earlier: being a part of the crowd vs. aligning oneself with the real laws of the market. Listening to propaganda – the endless chatter surrounding the market, believing countless "gurus" with agendas, a trader risks losing his individuality, his own understanding of events. It is one of the most important decisions in a trader's career: to separate himself from the myriad agendas pushed on him. As far as opinions go, most of them are simply a self-serving propaganda. Also, often there is no easy way to discern the market guru with real knowledge from the one who has none – if anything, most of them possess the ability to sound convincing. A trader can align himself with the market signals and become free from the endless chatter produced by those who don't have his best interests at heart. Making this choice and listening to market information flow instead of the surrounding noise frees a trader from those harmful external influences. A Taoist Trader can actually make those influences useful as he compares them to real market events and finds out what kind of agenda is being propagated by the actors. Understanding the purposes of such misinformation allows a trader to act in his best interests by both, avoiding becoming a victim of deception and utilizing the understanding of the deceiver's purpose. Obviously in order to do this a trader needs to learn the market language. While commentators talk to their audience in plain language, the market speaks in its own – language of prints on the tape; buys and sells, bids and offers.

Comparing external information and market events is one of the most powerful weapons in a trader's arsenal. Seeing upgrades and rosy announcements for the company whose stocks had a big run-up prior to this wave of positive noise is not a reason to buy for an astute trader – that would be an action of the one influenced by propaganda. If, however, observing the price action on such stock, a trader sees lower prices and selling pressure in response to upgrades – such negative divergence immediately puts him on alert. Seeing an agenda aimed at supporting the bidding for a stock, sending new buyers in it while a lot of shares are being sold, our trader knows the attempt to pump the stock is afoot. In accordance with market information he will turn bearish on such stock or at the very least will refrain from buying it. Obviously, the same pattern of price and information divergence will hold for the market sectors or market as a whole.

In the same way, a wise trader will be on watch for the avalanche of negative information about certain market sectors or companies while price action would not confirm the negative bias. This situation will put him on alert for bullish action, or at least staying away from shorting. In both cases, it is a conscious choice to align oneself with forces of market, just as a Taoist aligns himself with the forces of Nature, which enables a trader to stay on the right side.

Another trading application of the spokes-and-wheel stanza concerns a trader's perception of a certain trading situation he has seen before. Oftentimes, an experienced trader acts in a recognizable situation automatically, following a familiar string of steps as a response to a familiar market action. It is imperative to make such response truly automatic in order to avoid repetitive thinking over the same situation. Such thinking is slowing down a trader's response. It also carries a danger of seeing non-existent or insignificant differences and having second thoughts about the right course of action. The slogan "This time it's different" is not called the most dangerous for nothing. Standard situation requires standard, and not a creative, response. Perceiving such situations (setups) as spokes with no individuality and treating them as such, guarantees a quick automatic reaction that is aligned with market patterns. Such reactions will guarantee a winning in a statistically valid number of samples, while attempt to creatively treat every situation as individual will lead to random results.

Yet another trading application we need to touch: being guided by major principles vs. temporary structures. A consistent trader has his robust trading system designed, tested and proven. Now and then, however, additional opportunities arise from certain inefficiencies caused by imbalances such as un-coordinated pricing between exchanges or lag in trading technology allowing more advanced party to take an advantage of another. While this kind of inefficiencies can sometimes offer spectacular opportunities, they are usually short-lived as inefficiency becomes obvious quickly and the window of opportunity closes rapidly. An example of such temporary chances can be seen in arbitrage plays between different markets created by rapid technology advances – this was the case for electronic communication networks (ECNs) in the beginning of 2000s. These kinds of profits are provided by tricks rather than by a solid system, and tricks work only for so long. While a trader should not dismiss such opportunities when they arise, he is still advised to remember that it will be short-lived; thus he should not focus on it as much as to make it his main method of making a living. When the door closes, a solid trader simply returns to doing what he was always doing, while those not distinguishing between a real trading system and temporary tricks suffer the consequences of their short-sightedness.

Mold clay into a vessel;
From its not-being (in the vessel's hollow)
Arises the utility of the vessel.
Cut out doors and windows in the house (-wall),
From their not-being (empty space) arises the utility of the house.

Seeing "both sides of the coin" is one of a trader's tools for remaining objective and balanced. It is the key to flexibility and adaptability. Being emotionally invested in a certain market direction will distort our objectivity and make us substitute wishful thinking for reality. Thus it is beneficial to look at the chart from the point of view of having an opposite position – short if you are long, or contemplating long entry, and vice-versa. View from the other side will lend you objectivity as you will be able to see whether taking a trade in opposite direction looks attractive, or what conditions, should you enter the trade in one direction would trigger you to reverse your stance.

Just like Nature, markets have a natural flow which sometimes gets blocked by an intervention of some specific interests. Such blockage often creates a window of opportunity for an observant trader. The breach of a block usually resolves in a rapid turbulent move, as force accumulated by an artificial obstacle empties out briskly. A break of a particularly strong resistance or support often leads to such rapid movement – break of a consolidation range trades are based on this principle. Unusually big bid or offer can also serve as a something to watch for – when taken out, it often is a sign of an immediate brisk move.

Don't confuse a blockage of flow with a stall caused by lack of interest. In the former case you will see a lot of volume at a certain level without price movement. Such situation is charged with a brisk movement after the "lid is lifted". The latter case will be illustrated by a very low volume; while such a situation will present opportunities when some event brings interest back, it can take a long and unknown time for this event to happen and there is no point in tying up your attention.

Therefore by the existence of things we profit.
And by the non-existence of things we are served.

The last stanza is a traditional Taoist warning. We "profit" by attending to our interests and making sure that as traders we stay objective and goal-oriented. We "are served" by not being obedient listeners to "gurus" with agendas. A practical example of this duality is an attitude toward shorting. As traders we know that both directions are necessary for the market and that trading in both directions is only natural and required when the requisite conditions present themselves. There are circles, however, that try to present a point of view of shorting as "anti-patriotic". Another example of imposing unrelated values on traders is mixing in a social element by suggesting that some companies are worth trading and some are not depending on their social roles. Obviously as far as trading for profit is concerned, you are interested in success – and your success is determined by your skill in reading the price movements and utilizing them. Evidently circles promoting the notions of shorting being anti-patriotic or mixing social responsibility into trading do not hold our best interests in heart and listening to them we would be ill-served.

12.
The Senses

The five colors blind the eyes of man;
The five musical notes deafen the ears of man;
The five flavors dull the taste of man;
Horse-racing, hunting and chasing madden the minds
Of man;
Rare, valuable goods keep their owners
awake at night.
Therefore the Sage:
Provides for the belly and not for the eye.
Hence, he rejects the one and accepts the other.

The five senses: hearing, sight, taste, touch and smell, serve as the window through which we perceive the world. Our brains use the information provided by these receptors to analyze their input and make decisions based on models and frameworks by which we conduct our lives. These same receptors, however, can be and are used to submit false information and create reality-distorting models in our minds.

The five colors blind the eyes of man;
The five musical notes deafen the ears of man;
The five flavors dull the taste of man;

As soon as we start interacting with others, indoctrination starts. The concept of what is "good" and what is "bad" takes shape as information, in the form of values, enters first from our parents, then TV, friends and school. These concepts define what we want and desire – and those wants in turn become the governing principles guiding our behavior. In a way, our senses become" co-conspirators" and participate in this on-going programming that blinds us to reality. The effect of these external influences is the central theme of Senses.

Horse-racing, hunting and chasing madden the minds
of man;

Another common theme throughout the Tao Te Ching is a warning against pursuing societal goals that neither align with our talents nor our true desires; this line warns us against exceeding our personal limitations in pursuit of things beyond what is needed for true personal contentment. An internal conflict between our desires and actual needs is governed, to a large degree, by the external influences imposing on us the image of success. The idea of going beyond the requirements of our daily needs is identified by Lao Tzu as "attention to the externals." Conversely, "attention to the internals" is defined as building spiritual and philosophical principles that meet our daily needs so that our life may be more content. Taoism does not require one to abandon material possessions – it rather warns about the problem that arises when we sacrifice too much daily enjoyment for the idea of accumulating money and possessions.

Being encouraged by society to work ever harder and accumulate more material goods, the Taoist can counter this effect by asking "Why? Do I really want or need more stuff?" and "Am I doing this for my daily life or because of what society tells me I should have?"

It is exactly this type of perpetual societal propaganda that Taoism identifies as degrading our ability to evaluate how to conduct our lives. This is what Lao Tzu means in the poetry by ***"blinding the eyes," "deafening the ear," "dulling the taste," and "maddening the minds of man."***

Rare, valuable goods keep their owners awake at night.

The process of accumulating and hoarding wealth often becomes more important than using it to secure daily needs and a more content today. This focuses "attention to the externals," ***"keep(ing) their owners awake at night,"*** *worrying about guarding their valuables rather than using them. Basically, accumulation, possession, and fear of loss kill the joy of present moment, the one possession worth treasuring – the one of which you can accumulate no more – Time.*

Therefore the Sage:
Provides for the belly and not for the eye.
Hence, he rejects the one and accepts the other.

In this famous stanza, the "belly" and "eye" are an analogy to explain the struggle of "internal, daily needs" versus "external, future desires." Food for the belly is a concrete daily need. The eye sees images of many desirable objects, invoking the desire to chase socially promoted ideas of material desires. Hence, the Sage rejects social programming (the eye) that confuses our senses making us willing participants in the race for material goods and fame. Instead, he challenges himself to "provide for the belly."

PROPAGANDA in the markets takes many forms. It's delivered daily through all channels of information – newspapers, TV, Internet. It pushes all kinds of misinformation on market participants – new sensational trading systems promising quick riches; convincing sounding opinions about the market direction; promotion of certain stocks and sectors. An astute trader knows that these kinds of external influences must be verified against what the market itself says. He blocks such influences from impacting his trading decisions or even uses them in order to understand in which direction the crowd is manipulated. His sense of reality provides him with a compass allowing him to navigate the seas of propaganda.

Hearing about great new trading system that will provide a buyer with secrets to immense riches for $29.95, a wise trader will ask himself: Why would anyone sell it at all if it existed? How can it work if it's so accessible that it can be bought by literally everyone with the equivalent of a one–day's salary at McDonalds? Who would all these prospects for unlimited riches take the money from if winning is guaranteed for anyone using this sure system?

Being told by means of a mass e-mail about a great opportunity coming in some stock, he will ask why a sender wants all the recipients of e-mail to buy the stock. Framed in the right way, such questions will provide the right answer: it's all propaganda – misinformation taking different shapes. Most importantly, this false information is extremely harmful for those who take it at face value and act accordingly.

From the moment a person gets interested in financial markets, misinformation starts. It aims to create an outlook that serves interests of many entities in financial world – much less so interests of an individual. "In the long run markets always go up", "markets can't be timed", "start investing early and add regularly", "let the professionals manage your money" – if it all sound familiar, it very well should. Promising financial security with no effort applied, these slogans lure people into trusting their money to those who are not being paid for their effectiveness managing money. It doesn't take much to see how flawed the reasoning is:

- inflation erases the proceeds of the market gains in long run;
- market goes up for you "in a long run" only if you get lucky to start investing during the cycle's low and withdraw your funds at the cycle's high;
- if you continue investing regularly and go through a few up and down cycles, you average cost will largely eliminate the gains – still leaving you vulnerable to inflation;
- if your professional money manager puts your funds into particular companies, market gain may not be of much benefit for you as indexes get reshuffled regularly with underperforming companies being replaced by better performers;
- if markets can't be timed, then what do professional traders do every day buying and selling stocks?

  Rejecting such indoctrination and guarding himself against external influence, a trader stays independent, protects himself from manipulators' agendas and stays true to the real laws of the markets.

There is a natural limit to profits that can be made with relative safety in the market. Attempts to push beyond such limits expose a trader to a bigger risk jeopardizing his working capital and his very survival. According to Taoism's warning against chasing material possessions advertised by society rather than needed for his daily life, a trader should control his risk tightly and avoid chasing improbable profits. No single trade should be done with position size carrying potential risk of destroying a trader's account – no matter how luring the profit is. It's is destructive to one's trading and to his emotional balance. It is a well known effect of losing ability to sleep when one's exposure to the market exceeds his risk tolerance (***Rare, valuable goods keep their owners awake at night.***) Such emotional imbalance is a sure sign of taking an unreasonable risk. Keeping in line with idea of "providing for the belly and not for the eye" a trader stays within rational limits, controls his risk tight enough to guarantee long-term survival and preserves his daily contentment.

13.
Praise and Blame

Favor and disgrace cause one dismay;
"What we value and what we fear are within our Self."
What does this mean:
"Favor and disgrace cause one dismay?"
Those who receive a favor from above
Are dismayed when they receive it,
And dismayed when they lose it.
What does this mean:
"What we value and what we fear are within our Self?"
We have fears because we have a self.
When we do not regard that self as self,
What have we to fear?
Therefore he who values the world as his self
May then be entrusted with the government of the world;
And he who loves the world as his self -
The world may then be entrusted to his care.

In Praise and Blame, Lao Tzu, as he often does, speaks to how societal indoctrination forms our beliefs, and how to prioritize our values to maximize contentment. He uses the principle of Yin and Yang to explain how the definition of "Self" serves as a starting point for evaluating our progress along our Path.

"Praise and blame" and "favor and disgrace," are determined by what we consider to be good or bad. We receive praise and favor for doing "Good" and are blamed or punished for doing "Bad." Good and bad, success and failure, right and wrong, are defined by the values of the society in which we live. Society propagates and reinforces these values through rewards and punishments via various civic and legal institutions. The messages of those institutions are also communicated by media – books, magazines, movies, television, and music. The societal model for happiness is codified in the description of an ideal citizen that we are urged to emulate, and his possessions we are urged to desire.

We know that value systems are constructed to benefit society as a whole, not the individual. Since society consists of individuals with varying wants, needs and abilities, values of the group are often radically different than those benefiting the individual. Thus, the Tao Te Ching emphasizes the potentially devastating impact of value systems on individual contentment.

Throughout history, values have been in constant flux. Changing values cause confusion in the mind of individuals, discontent and suffering. If values change, they are not, by definition, principles. Over time, shifting values, like shifting sand on which the house is built, will cause stress and the foundation will break. To the Taoist, principles for life's guide should be based on observable phenomena, proven manifestations, and should provide a solid foundation that function at all times.

What does this mean:
"Favor and disgrace cause one dismay?"

Society's definitions of good and bad describe behaviors which are of "favor" or "disgrace" which work against the individual and "cause dismay." A metaphor to visualize this view is a "values shirt." The shirt is made of different threads, in which each thread represents a different value. All the threads are woven together to create a shirt good-looking but of a single size for everyone. However, since people come in all shapes and sizes, it fits some individuals better than others. The people it fits are praised for how good it looks on them. Those for whom the shirt doesn't fit so well will have to cram themselves into it, or the shirt will hang off them. Not being able to fit into the shirt like others will cause them dismay. They are going to feel like misfits, eventually resenting themselves or society.

Those who receive a favor from above
Are dismayed when they receive it,
And dismayed when they lose it.

It's fairly obvious why disgrace, the inability to meet society's expectations, would cause dismay. However, those who have been blessed with society's favor ("receive a favor from above") also are often dismayed. There are numerous examples of success stories not bringing happiness, and turning into disaster. One primary reason for this is the anxiety that one can never have enough of that which bestows favor. The individual engages in an endless treadmill run to acquire more, while cradling possessions that can be lost – and the concomitant suffering that accompanies the fear of loss. The more one has, the more one must have and the more time must be devoted to maintaining those possessions. So you end up "dismayed when you receive" and "dismayed when you lose."

The second disconnect between success and happiness is in the belief that possessions are the key to success and happiness. They however are meant to be the means to the end, not the end itself.

What does this mean:
"What we value and what we fear are within our Self?"
We have fears because we have a self.

Our ability to meet the standards imposed by the society weighs on our minds. Our "Self" becomes our identity which we compare with the external model provided by society; we fret about being able to emulate this model.

When we do not regard that self as self,
What have we to fear?

Here, Lao Tzu defines how the individual should set his priorities for life by recognizing that we have a physical Self (our body) and a non-physical Self (the soul). He suggests giving priority to nourishing the soul, as the body is only a temporary vessel. As the home for the soul, however, the body must be cared for. Chuang Tzu commented that: "The perfect man ignores self; the divine man ignores achievement; the true Sage ignores reputation." Taoism reminds us that our physical life is temporary – the trappings of success will be left behind at death – as will the societal values we held so dear. This reduces the fear and dismay caused by society's artificial goals as their temporary nature diminishes their importance. However, we still desire a comfortable life, even if temporary. Thus, our challenge is to avoid taking society's urgings to heart by deciding what amount of possessions are necessary and enough for contentment. Too much sacrifice for material possessions wastes energy and brings fear of loss. Similarly, too much sacrifice for uncertain heavenly rewards can cause discontent now. Thus, the Taoist must find the fine balance between opposing states to achieve harmony.

Therefore he who values the world as his self
May then be entrusted with the government of the world;
And he who loves the world as his self -
The world may then be entrusted to his care.

Much of the Tao Te Ching was written for China's rulers and government officials. True principles that work for governing oneself, will also work for governing a state. A government that provides for both the material needs of its citizens plus gives them the freedom to develop their souls is to be "trusted." Similarly, the Founders when framing the Constitution of the United States included the principles of self-interest, free thinking without government control, laissez-faire domestic and foreign policies, and a system of checks and balances to limit state interference.

What we value and what we fear are within our Self

THERE are two aspects to this stanza. First, this is a reminder that a trader is not performing his tasks for anyone's entertainment or to earn someone's praise. It's a slippery slope to try and voice one's opinion to win public sympathy and earn popularity among followers. This does nothing but feeds a trader's Ego – and when Ego is involved, there is no place for humility. Being in the public eye, a trader risks getting locked in his published opinion and stubbornly defending it in the face of the market telling him/her otherwise. Many capable traders, while performing admirably in trading for themselves, failed spectacularly when trying to make their opinions public. The underlying reason for this phenomenon is an attempt to satisfy some external audience, instead of being "one's own person." Even as simple an action as posting one's opinion on a market or particular stock direction can serve as a hindrance in one's trading, as he feels obliged to "stay the course." A Taoist Trader keeps his views to himself and trades based on those views; he is not subjected to external influences, does not allow his Ego to spring into action, thus remaining humble and willing to accept being wrong on the spot. Such humility keeps him flexible, free to follow the market's whims and sensitive to the changes in trends in the trading environment. He embraces such changes as his normal surroundings instead of being caught unprepared by them.

The second aspect is the concept of our inner world, our mindset, our character traits and self-control being determining factors in our trading success. Many beginning traders attribute their success or failure to external factors – blaming the market, its powerful and sinister participants, commentators or analysts. More seek success in a "secret" winning trading system, "magic" indicator, hidden from the public formula for profitable trading etc. Notice how many websites sell their useless get-rich-quick schemes using words "secret", "never published before" or claiming that "professionals are angry at us for revealing this powerful technique." Of course there are no secrets; the scheme was never published because there was nothing to publish and real professionals never even heard of the technique being revealed with such pomp. Trading systems that work are well known, described in numerous books and articles and for the most part are fairly simple. The problem that traders encounter is not finding the system or choosing the indicator– none of them guarantees success by itself. The real problem is the ability to apply any system with strict discipline and strong self-control. It's not learning the rules where we fail – it's following them. Our behavior is not necessary rational and governed by logic and pursuing our best interests. More often it's dictated by emotions, distorted perception and wishful thinking. Thus, it is our inner self that is the major obstacle on the path to trading success. This is why traders applying the same system will produce different results – even though the system is the same, they will apply it differently. Some will act in a more disciplined fashion; some will violate the rules when they feel they know better; some won't be able to avoid sabotaging themselves by giving in to temptations of the Ego, fear, greed and/or wishful thinking.

Those who advance on the way of learning far enough realize that to become successful traders they need to learn about themselves and change themselves. They understand the need to know themselves well – to know their strengths and weaknesses, to foresee the situations in which they are likely to succeed as well as fail. Such knowledge creates a foundation for the next step – changing their inner workings, cultivating helpful traits and weeding out harmful ones; in other words developing and evolving the trader within. This process of adjusting, of self-change is the most important part of the process of learning to trade.

"Favor and disgrace cause one dismay"
Those who receive a favor from above
Are dismayed when they receive it,
And dismayed when they lose it.

As we said earlier, a trader is not performing his tasks to earn someone's praise. As his own person, he simply tries to stay in tune with the market and act on his read. Attempts to impress external audiences can be equally ruinous whether he succeeds or not. Praise from his listeners raises his Ego, creates and reinforces the need to give them more and to hear more commendations. Instead of speaking only when there is something about which to speak, a trader risks speaking for speaking's sake – just to keep his audience "informed" and entertained. Negative feedback from the audience can be devastating for a trader's self-esteem; and can easily create anger, animosity and feelings of inadequacy. It can push him to unneeded arguments over nothing; such fights are colossal wastes of time and energy. In attempts to vindicate himself he is likely to engage in even more defensive actions, trying to prove himself to total strangers. All this is unproductive, emotionally debilitating and destructive.

A Taoist Trader will continue trading and consider his success in the market the only proof of competency he needs. If he has the need to express his point of view, he will not argue or defend it if met with animosity – he will leave it to his listeners to sort things out and accept or dismiss his opinion. He will answer the honest question but won't be dragged into wasteful quarrelling. Winning a verbal argument has no value for him; he realizes that Ego satisfaction is the only result of such a victory, and it is not what he is after.

We have fears because we have a self.
When we do not regard that self as self,
What have we to fear?

Trading activity is aimed at making money. However, in a paradoxical way, a trader performs much better when he is not focused on making money. Concentrating on the monetary aspect of his action creates fear – a paralyzing and debilitating state of mind where a trader's actions are governed by the desire to protect his profit and avoid a loss. Such motives, seemingly correct, in reality are harmful as they encourage a trader to act based on his monetary circumstances and not on what the market is telling him. As a result, he is likely to take a small profit out of fear of letting it evaporate – even though the market never generated a sell signal. Similarly, he is likely to take a loss or sell his position breakeven long before the market signaled that a trade is not going to work. Such behavior ruins the odds upon which the trading system is built. Instead of acting on valid and true signals from the market, the trader acts on noise – small accidental movements that have no meaning. Sometimes a simple action such as removing the profit/loss column from one's screen ("**not regard(ing) that self as self**") helps disassociate a trader from his monetary results and allows him to focus on the right thing, the real subject of his work – the market movements. It breaks the mental link between his action and money, helping alleviate the fear and remove the influence of emotions.

Therefore he who values the world as his self
May then be entrusted with the government of the world;
And he who loves the world as his self -
The world may then be entrusted to his care.

For a wise skillful trader with an advanced understanding of markets, trading becomes a natural part of his life. He sees trading activity as one manifestation of the world's natural order; to him, it's no longer some separate activity with its own rules and laws. He understands the analogies and interconnections between the natural laws that govern all things around him and those of the market. He can see clearly how Tao, the natural law according to which everything works, manifests itself in trading just as in any other life phenomena. He no longer contrasts himself with the rest of market participants or the market itself; instead he becomes an inalienable part of it (**values the world as his self.**) Being one with market helps him understand its movements, changes and intentions; he flows naturally with the market as a solitary leaf rides with the river's current. The market ceases to be a hostile environment for the trader; it becomes his habitat that does not instill fear, feels respectful and deserving respect. A trader becomes as accustomed to this environment as he is to his own home. This mental state alleviates stress – unlike many beginning traders, a Taoist trader is not at war with the market anymore. At the same time, he never feels complacent and careless – he respects the market just as he respects Nature and its immense power. He is not unlike an experienced captain of a seafaring ship, who feels at home in the middle of the ocean, who acts with confidence and has firm control over fear, yet never loses a healthy respect for the forces of Nature and remains careful at all times.

14.
Prehistoric Origins

Looked at, but cannot be seen --
That is called the Invisible (yi).
Listened to, but cannot be heard --
That is called the Inaudible (hsi).
Grasped at, but cannot be touched --
That is called the Intangible (wei).
These three elude all our inquiries.
And hence blend and become One.
Not by its rising, is there light,
Not by its sinking, is there darkness.
Unceasing, continuous,
It cannot be defined,
And reverts again to the realm of nothingness.
That is why it is called the Form of the Formless.
The Image of Nothingness.
That is why it is called the Elusive,
Meet it and you do not see its face,
Follow it and you do not see its back.
He who holds fast to the Tao of old,
In order to manage the affairs of Now
Is able to know the Primeval Beginnings,
Which are the continuity of Tao.

A recurring theme of the Tao Te Ching is the necessity to accept our personal limitations, be it physical ones (how much we can lift, or how fast we can run), intellectual ones (our ability to do mathematical calculations in our head), or metaphysical – limits to our abilities to know about what happens in the matters usually classified as "spiritual."

Our lifetime is but speck of time compared to the lifespan of the Universe. This limitation carries many implications, for without knowledge of the time before birth or after death, every moment on earth is precious. The urgency of learning is compounded by the fact that death can come unexpectedly.

The very title of this poem, "Prehistoric Origins," is a reminder about our temporal limitations. The Tao exists outside of time as we know it; it pre-dates any definable beginning and is older than the Universe. This origin touches another aspect of our limitations -- we can only contemplate things that we can define, the Tao exceeds anything describable with words.

Trying to understand the Tao through observation we infer that the world around us operates on a set of principles; we however cannot comprehend their operation. We can observe the phenomenon of gravity and label it as such, but giving it a name does not mean we really understand it. We name principles, measure them, even create formulas to predict their action; however, we cannot see the underlying system that brings them into being. We also see that the world is consistent – gravity works today just as it did yesterday and probably will do tomorrow. We thus recognize, through experience, that the world is a system, with underlying rules; the totality of the system however is beyond our comprehension.

We call the system, the Tao, and the manifestations of that system, Te. Since the manifestations are all we can see, we study them in order to learn about the underlying system. This is not idle intellectual curiosity; greater understanding how a system behaves decreases the danger of becoming its victim.

Looked at, but cannot be seen --
That is called the Invisible (yi).
Listened to, but cannot be heard --
That is called the Inaudible (hsi).
Grasped at, but cannot be touched --
That is called the Intangible (wei).
These three elude all our inquiries.
And hence blend and become One.

*The Tao, the law according to which everything happens, **"cannot be seen"** – only its manifestations (Te) are visible. Nature exhibits Taoist principles. The Tao is undetectable by our senses: **"cannot be seen"**, **"cannot be heard"** and **"cannot be touched."** The Tao cannot be perceived directly. We don't know the source of the things around us, and their destination is uncertain for us. We however can analyze the manifestations of the Tao and make certain conclusions about the forces in action, thus arming ourselves with tool necessary for navigating our way in the world.*

Not by its rising, is there light,
Not by its sinking, is there darkness.
Unceasing, continuous,
It cannot be defined,
And reverts again to the realm of nothingness.

*Daylight is caused by the presence of the sun, and darkness – by its absence; the sun itself a manifestation of the Tao. All the phenomena of the world come and go, while the Tao itself is "**unceasing.**" The system is always present ("**continuous**"), as are the processes of creation and destruction.*

Our finite natures make a quest to find the Tao impossible. There is no benefit in attempting to answer unanswerable questions. Obsessing over questions we are simply not equipped to answer is a waste of precious time. Instead, it is important to keep ourselves grounded in reality, dealing with issues we can actually comprehend. Our finite lifetimes mean there is an urgency to find contentment in the present.

That is why it is called the Form of the Formless.
The Image of Nothingness.

*The Tao itself is not material and thus has no form – it only governs the forms of material objects. Having no visible form that our limited intellect and perception can detect; it is the source of the various material things that we can sense. Through perceiving them and observing their interaction we can get an "**Image of Nothingness.**"*

That is why it is called the Elusive,
Meet it and you do not see its face,
Follow it and you do not see its back.

*The Tao seems "**elusive**" because it defies any attempt we make to see it. As a manifestation of Tao, we can see it directly no more than a steering wheel can see and understand how the whole automobile works. Whatever we see is material and thus simply a manifestation.*

He who holds fast to the Tao of old,
In order to manage the affairs of Now
Is able to know the Primeval Beginnings,
Which are the continuity of Tao.

*Although the material world changes, the Tao does not. Nor can we change it or how it operates – attempts to impose our own design on it are doomed to fail. To "**hold fast**" to the old means to recognize the truth of underlying laws that define how the world works.*

*The Taoist sees himself as part of the continuous stream of change that occurs in the material world. He recognizes that all material things are transitory, and that everything is in a constant state of flux. He recognizing these changes to be inevitable and simply adapts to them ("**manage the affairs of Now.**")*

*The emphasis on "**Now**" in this line of poetry is Lao Tzu's caution against putting too much faith in planning or expectations for the future. A recurring theme in the Tao Te Ching is the futility of excessive planning. We can do well if we clearly see what is happening now and remembering that we have no ability to foresee the future.*

Looked at, but cannot be seen --
That is called the Invisible (yi).
Listened to, but cannot be heard --
That is called the Inaudible (hsi).
Grasped at, but cannot be touched --
That is called the Intangible (wei).
These three elude all our inquiries.
And hence blend and become One.

THE market moves through the dynamic interaction of opposing forces – one of buying and one of selling. While the resulting direction is defined by the more powerful (at the moment) side, there is no direct way to determine which of them is more powerful and by how much. Many traders attempt to predict the direction using differing analyses; some of them make the mistake of trying to find out everything about the moving forces hoping to arrive at an absolute conclusion. Such attempts are doomed to fail. Underlying forces moving the market are too large and numerous for a single person to comprehend, and most importantly – they do not remain static. As the price changes so do intentions – new motivations appear while old ones get discarded; new plans are contemplated; new entities become interested and join the game; unrelated factors influence decisions, etc, etc.

If major forces moving the market could be seen directly they would never be able to accomplish their task. Their attempts to buy would be front-run by those who try to get on the bandwagon, and the sellers would back away, raising prices and refusing to sell cheap to a large accumulating player. Their attempt to sell would be undercut by those who want out before it's too late and lower their offers, and the buyers would have canceled their bids and refused to buy until a significant price drop. The whole market continuum would have been ruined – IF underlying forces could be seen directly. The effective force is one that cannot be seen.

A Taoist trader realizes that if a situation arises where a certain direction or market event becomes obvious – it's likely to be a trap for those who naively think the market can be that obvious. In order for someone to win there must be someone to take an opposite side of the trade and be mistaken – who and why would have taken the opposite side if things were so obvious? If some event is so palpable that everyone can foresee it, there is practically no chance the expected move would not occur in advance of such an event. In other words, tomorrow's events are accounted for by today's price action. This is how the market frustrates those who adopt a simple-minded approach, expecting the market to act logically, in a simplistic straightforward manner. They see what lies right in front of them and expect the market to act according to that evident factor. What they don't realize is that if it's evident to them, it's evident to everyone – thus cannot be actionable because everyone cannot win. There simply won't be anyone to take the other side of their trades – why would anyone sell if it's obvious to all players that the price must go up? Similarly, no one is going to buy if it's obvious that the price is going to drop.

Seeing someone buying in the face of an obviously "inevitable" price drop, and seeing the price held steady by that "someone," a trader understanding the Taoist principles will see a bear trap ready to close on those who sell. Seeing someone selling in the face of obviously "inevitable" price rise, and seeing the price held steady by that "someone," a trader understanding the Taoist principles will see a bull trap ready to close on those who buy. Understanding that the obvious cannot work in the markets becomes the most powerful weapon in a trader's arsenal. He will look for situations where certain information leads to obvious conclusions, yet the price action contradicts the obvious – and position himself on the side of the price, against the obvious.

A Taoist Trader understands that the move is more likely to occur before the event connected to this move becomes widely known. Thus instead of attempting to find out what underlying reasons and forces do to influence market movement, the odds of the certain direction can be read more reliably through the manifestation of those forces: As they position themselves for the move, they leave certain tracks. Their buying and selling allows qualifying their action as accumulation or distribution. Increasing or decreasing volume during price advance or retreat allows judging the path of the least resistance. Quiet orderly accumulation or distribution without sharp movements attracting attention is the sign of a large smart force in action. Noticing such methodical action, a trader will align himself with the direction, and wait for an event becoming known to the whole world. The resulting sharp hysterical movements will signal exit for the smart money that positioned itself in advance; our trader will close his position at this point as well, leaving those who trade the obvious wondering why the market reversed on them.

All over Internet you can observe traders trying to find out everything possible about a particular company, sector, industry, technology or product. In their quest for more and more information, they forget about the real purpose of their research. Instead of finding out the likely path of price action, they try to become specialists in a certain field, seek consults from those who work in the industry and try to stitch pieces of information together to create a complete picture. They hope that if they speak to a doctor about some new drug or technology designed by the company they research, professional insight will help them predict the future. More often than not it turns into a waste of time and leads them to false conclusions. Quick evaluation given by a doctor as an afterthought during a friendly dinner does not present a serious professional opinion. Even more troublesome is "group research" done by a crowd of strangers exchanging their opinions in some Internet forum. An assortment of people with unknown motivations or qualifications, with no confirmed track record or credentials – hard to think of a more dubious source of information for trading decisions. This entire quest for more and more information is a colossal waste of time, caused by the lack of understanding of an important Taoist principle: the impossibility to find out everything and chart your way with absolute certainty. It doesn't mean the research is not needed, but there should be a point of "necessary and sufficient." Also, sources must be considered and verified – anonymous communication over the Internet leaves too much room for propagating questionable information.

It is important for a trader to realize that being a part of the market, being one of participants, he is one of the manifestations of market forces too. If he wants to understand how other players think, feel and react, he needs to observe his own thoughts, feelings and reactions. When he experiences paralyzing fear, false hope or extreme elation, chances are those same emotions form the psyche of may others. Seeing those emotions in himself, he can use them as a window into the mindset of other participants. This self-observing process gives him the distance necessary for a more effective self-control and helps him understand what moves other market players. Emotions observed in such detached manner become duller and easier to control. When a trader forms a solid understanding of the reactions that make traders lose money and reactions that help them win, he becomes capable of recognizing the same reactions in himself and controls upon which impulses he acts. Such recognition of oneself as a part of the market is a very powerful weapon in learning both oneself and others. This approach allows a trader to lift himself above the crowd and establish a higher level of understanding and self-control.

He who holds fast to the Tao of old,
In order to manage the affairs of Now
Is able to know the Primeval Beginnings,
Which are the continuity of Tao.

Real forces creating market movements are the laws describing how changes occur; laws of Nature and laws of mass psychology. They are not material and they do not change. They create material forms, and they must be studied and understood in order to understand the forms they influence. Focusing on learning these laws is much more productive than focusing on minute changes themselves. A trader who derives his conclusions from the fundamental laws operates on much deeper level. He is not confused by insignificant changes that seem important only because they are right in front of us.

Picture a sharp spike in the price of a stock just featured on CNBC. A trader taking such promotion at face value will buy the stock and hold it in the hope that all the wonderful things said in the TV profile materialize in the stock price. A Taoist Trader understands that such a miniscule event is insignificant in the big picture, and as soon as the short-lived enthusiasm dissipates, a stock will return to its normal patterns and its price will move governed by market laws and trends. If his time frame is larger than intraday movements, he will ignore this event altogether. If he is a short-term trader, he will take advantage of rapid price change. By no means however will he allow himself to get caught in hype and abandon his general understanding for the momentary excitement. Be it a TV profile, an analysts upgrade or article in a printed publication, the mechanics of public reaction is the same.

Knowing that the major laws ruling the market changes do not change themselves, the Taoist trader will look for similarities in any new market environment. Immediate participants in any market event, significant or not, tend to overstate the differences they observe. It makes them think they encounter something no one has ever seen before. Such a position leaves them helpless as they have no frame of reference. Thinking that they navigate uncharted waters, they fail to see how the same eternal laws govern this "new" environment. Attempting to act on this "new paradigm", they ignore the real market patterns and take positions against them. Acting like this, a trader goes against two principles described in this Taoist poem. The first error is ignoring the everlasting market laws in favor of the momentary situation. Second error is thinking that market movements can be predicted with certainty, and his understanding is the only right one with which the market will have to fall in step. Such behavior ends in inevitable frustration and loss. Almost invariably as the market proves him wrong, he blames his losses on manipulation, on sinister forces and their deceptive practices. Such explanations help him preserve his Ego as he portrays himself a victim of menacing omnipotent manipulators. It may very well help him feel better but serves no useful purpose as far as profitable trading goes. All this will result in frustration and anger, but never in productive action. There is a good reason for the phrase "This time it's different" to be called the most expensive one in human history.

Not by its rising, is there light,
Not by its sinking, is there darkness.

Unceasing, continuous,
It cannot be defined,
And reverts again to the realm of nothingness.

Finally, speaking of the eternal laws of the market, we must touch again on market cycles. It is one of the most common mistakes to count on endless movement in the same direction, thinking that whatever we know about the economics, particular industry or company will make the price move forever, thus never taking profit. Think of how many "investors" never realized the technology boom of 1998-2000 was coming to an end, and continued talking about the "New Economy." Think of the most recent housing boom and how it caught so many off guards when it ended. The same happens during the downward movements – market reversal to the upside in March of 2009 followed by unrelenting upward move caught just as many trying to short the market all throughout the rally. Browsing the Internet, you could see countless bearish groups of traders rationalizing their point of view, insisting on initiating and holding short positions, expressing frustration and anger when proven wrong time and again. Once again, traders relied on their subjective and limited understanding, allowing their opinion to take over, triggering their Ego and making them stubbornly insist on their views, as if they were entitled to being right and being profitable.

Instead, a skillful trader, respecting market laws and staying sensitive to changes, would have abandoned the idea that he knows better. He would have focused on market action, trying to listen to what the market said. After such an extreme movement to the downside that occurred in previous months, he would be on the lookout for a trend reversal – because he knows that the market moves in cycles. Bullish phase yields to bearish one; cycle repeats when bearish phase gets exhausted. Throughout the whole cycle a Taoist trader observes those who press the trend change too early and those who stay with trend for too long. Both make the same mistake in different manifestations: they do not respect natural market forces, not giving them the right time to work themselves out. These traders believe in their ability to predict the future with no reservations or due humility. Such overconfidence is based on the erroneous idea that they can figure out the market with certainty; it leads them to a premature hunt for a trend reversal or to overstaying their welcome in trend direction.

How does the Taoist trader resolve this contradiction between staying in a trend and changing his bias? By realizing that he can not know with certainty all the underlying happenings; by dismissing external noise of news and opinions as irrelevant, and by listening to the market instead

When defining whether he stays with trend or not, he doesn't guess – he waits for the market to tell him that the trend has changed. Whatever method of reading he applies, he has a sign of trend change as a part of his trading system, and he watches for that sign to appear – be it a chart formation or technical indicator or candlestick signal. When uncertainty goes beyond his level of comfort, he lightens up on his position, thus controlling his risk. Acting this way he is likely to miss the exact reversal moment, and he is quite comfortable with it. He realizes that catching exact tops or bottoms is impossible; a traders' attempts to do so are the Ego manifesting itself. Instead, a wise trader waits for the market to give clear signals of the trend change, and closes his position. Alternatively, he may close his position when the risk rises beyond acceptable limits.

When determining whether its time to take a position in the opposite direction, an experienced trader doesn't guess either. He again waits for the market to tell him that the trend has changed. Once again, it is a signal in terms of his trading system that must be generated for him to take action. Once again, acting this way he is likely to miss the exact reversal moment, and he is quite comfortable with that. He is not likely to participate in the very beginning of the movement, and he is likely to miss the end of it – but the portion of the movement he can utilize is the easiest to read and less risky.

Such an approach satisfies Taoist principles. A trader acting this way:

- respects market cycles;
- doesn't attempt to outsmart the market;
- listens to market signals;
- stays sensitive to the changes, and
- aligns his action with natural everlasting laws governing the market.

15.
The Wise Ones of Old

The wise ones of old had subtle wisdom and depth of understanding,
So profound that they could not be understood.
And because they could not be understood,
Perforce must they be so described:
Cautious, like crossing a wintry stream,
Irresolute, like one fearing danger all around,
Grave, like one acting as guest,
Self-effacing, like ice beginning to melt,
Genuine, like a piece of undressed wood,
Open-minded, like a valley,
And mixing freely, like murky water.
Who can find repose in a muddy world?
By lying still, it becomes clear.
Who can maintain his calm for long?
By activity, it comes back to life.
He who embraces this Tao
Guards against being over-full.
Because he guards against being over-full,
He is beyond wearing out and renewal.

Skilled professionals demonstrate their abilities with practical accomplishments. In the same way, when one internalizes Taoist principles, actions should reflect mastery of the philosophy. Without action, any amount of intellectual or spiritual development is irrelevant. Lao Tzu insists action is the litmus test for proficiency.

The Tao Te Ching is comprehensive not only in its explanations of the Taoist's philosophical principles (encoded as they are), but also in describing the characteristics that an individual must display in his daily actions. The Wise Ones of Old lists seven characteristics the Sages personify.

1. Cautious, like crossing a wintry stream

We go through daily routine tasks with a casual level of attention and a low intensity focus. This laissez-faire attitude, while seemingly harmless in insignificant situations, cultivates bad habits. We recognize that wrong decision in a critical junction can be devastating; we are less likely to identify the dangers of less than optimum decision-making in seemingly benign situations.

Those sub-optimal decisions though have a cumulative effect. Over time, the collective missteps have a snowballing effect. Thus the Taoist approaches even the most routine tasks with caution and focus "like crossing a wintry stream."

Focused involvement and remaining mindful from moment to moment raises our awareness of our surroundings. It allows us to absorb subtle information from the environment and detect things undetectable to the casual observer. This ability to react on the developments as if they were foreseen is regarded by less experienced as supernatural.

2. *Irresolute, like one fearing danger all around*

Irresolute in this case rather means untrusting, or not trustful. One who fears "danger all around" means to be suspicious of surroundings. The Taoist is aware of conflicting self-interests of others and chaotic changes of circumstances beyond our control are constancies of life. Therefore he avoids making assumptions, stays alert to inconsistent details, and tries constantly to gauge whether the situation or individual warrants his trust.

3. *Grave, like one acting as guest*

As guests in someone's house or foreign land, our level of awareness should be elevated vs. one we exercise in the safe confines of home. In these situations, we apply a heightened state of alertness, carefully conduct ourselves and interact with others. Taoism prescribes acknowledging our status as temporary guests on this planet, thus instructing us to conduct ourselves with similar sensitivity and seriousness.

4. *Self-effacing, like ice beginning to melt*

Self-effacing behavior is based on humility. Its direct opposite, pride and arrogance, is the cause of many problems. Humility implies understanding and acknowledging our limitations. By recognizing our insufficient level of knowledge, we realize that we have much to learn and become open to absorbing the lessons of life.

Unassuming behavior also mitigates the antagonism of others. Boasting behavior provokes the resentment and animosity in those around us. Accomplished persons possess genuine humility and are held in high esteem by the virtue of their achievements, without showing off or drumming their chest.

5. *Genuine, like a piece of undressed wood*

"Undressed" or uncarved wood is Taoism's metaphor for an uncorrupted character." The idea is to restore our original nature. In this metaphor, the "undressed wood" represents our character before unnatural shaping by society takes place.

6. Open-minded, like a valley

The "valley" analogy refers to the openness of yin, or female, characteristics of our dualistic existence. A competitive environment promotes aggressive male qualities, including a more closed and rigid state of mind, less likely to accept new ideas or to adapt. By restoring a harmonious balance of yin and yang in our existence, we become more flexible. It allows us to switch from close-minded aggression to open-minded yielding when appropriate.

7. And mixing freely, like murky water

The Taoist adapts his behavior to the surrounding. Taoism does not advocate returning to Nature and living a tribal life. A proficient application of Taoism to one's life means the ability to carve out a content existence within a "murky" society.

Who can find repose in a muddy world?
By lying still, it becomes clear.
Who can maintain his calm for long?
By activity, it comes back to life.

*This stanza poses the question: How do you find serenity and peace in a world full of absurdity and chaos? The answer lies in embracing Taoist principles to identify and sort out the contradictions that cause confusion and discontentment. A dispassionate analytical process provides clear insight into events around us. With clarified vision, we can appropriately react to changing circumstances, allowing us to "**come back to life**."*

He who embraces this Tao
Guards against being over-full.
Because he guards against being over-full,
He is beyond wearing out and renewal.

*"**Over-full**" is another word for arrogance. The key to the meaning of this stanza is in the words "this Tao." Normally, in Taoist literature, "Tao" is written without qualification. The qualifier "this" in this poem reminds us that we can only see a small segment of the Tao. Being a part of Tao, one of its manifestations, we will never understand the entire system – to think so is to be "over-full." However, by recognizing that we can only see some of manifestations, ("this Tao,") we limit our quest to what can be comprehended and become less likely to "wear out" from life's hardships.*

SEVEN traits that characterize the Sage are just as applicable for a wise trader employing Taoism principles in his approach.

1. Cautious, like crossing a wintry stream

Trading becomes routine when technical aspects of it are mastered and a trader reaches a sufficient level of self-control. While this is a desirable state of mind that gives a trader the ability to remain calm and collected, there is, as is usually the case, another side to it. Settling into a routine, a trader tends to lose caution, relying too much on things remaining the same and continuing working as they did when his approach was bringing him success. Meanwhile, the market rarely stays the same for a prolonged period of time. Subtle changes accumulate, gradually preparing for a major change, abrupt or not. If a change happens in a sudden dramatic fashion, it can catch a trader off guard and cause sizeable losses. If a change occurs slowly and gradually, with no single event defining the sharp turn, it's even more dangerous as a trader sees his performance eroding slowly with no warning signs and with no clear recipe for what he needs to change in his approach. Worse yet, the performance will become weaker without the trader starting to worry at all – first stages of such erosion will seem to be just a natural variation. Thus, a significant part of the results worsening will pass by with a trader staying oblivious to the fact.

A Taoist Trader knows that things do not stay the same for very long. As comfortable as his routine is, he is always on the lookout for possible changes; he stays sensitive to subtle changes and he pays attention to the rising tension of equilibrium getting ready to shatter. A market staying locked in a very narrow range resolves into a sharp directional move; tightened Bollinger Bands indicate increases in volatility coming; a steady trend is followed by a sudden pullback; a chart pattern becoming too cozy suddenly stops working – all these are examples of a comfortable balance suddenly breaking down.

An experienced trader's readiness for such changes and his lightning reaction to them looks almost supernatural to the casual observer.

2. Irresolute, like one fearing danger all around

A trader understanding the markets will never view them as calm waters, to be trusted and relied upon. There is turbulence lurking under any seemingly smooth surface. The market is not a place of exchanging gifts and pouring herbal tea for a neighbor. There are many conflicting interests in a constant chain of collisions; sudden change can come about at any moment, and most likely when it's the least expected.

No statement is made without an agenda; no report is published without the authors' interests at heart. Each and every proclamation must be verified against market action. An astute trader will never act on information fed to him without making sure the market reacts in a way the information suggests. He will never make an automatic assumption that information is complete, correct and truthful. Offered trading advice, he will observe a particular market commentator first to gauge his skill, knowledge and honesty. Only after verifying an advisor's adequacy by comparing his forecasts to market action can he start acting on such advice.

Sometimes advice is given to newer traders to focus on a single stock and get familiar with the way it moves. A problem with this approach is that a trader starts feeling sometimes as if he developed a close relationship with a stock. He starts trusting it to "help him out". Meanwhile, the patterns he learned observing will not remain the same forever – some market events will influence a stock behavior. It wouldn't be a problem if a trader stayed alert and mistrustful – however making a single stock the only one he deals with can easily leave him defenseless as he develops "faith" in a stock. Similar problems can occur with trading a single sector or a single setup. Maintaining a healthy variety allows a trader to remain objective and emotionally detached.

3. Grave, like one acting as guest

Aside from the normal level of alertness in the market, a trader should go to a more elevated level when dealing with anything outside the norm. Earnings season presents a somewhat different environment; triple witching days introduce unusual factors; an IPO with no history is more challenging than an established stock. In all these situations a trader will diminish his expectations, control his risk especially tightly, and cut down the size of his positions.

Moving into a new trading vehicle (currencies, futures, options etc) is another example of a situation where a trader must feel himself as a guest, being especially careful. A trader will paper trade first, learning his new environment with no pressure of money on the line and no unjustified risk. In the same fashion, a new setup or strategy should be tested on paper or a simulator first.

Any new regulation can have deeper impacts than immediately obvious, as it changes motivations and capabilities of many market participants. Introduction of online discount brokers enabled home-based traders to become active market participants, changing the field for the whole industry. The appearance of "direct access" brokers armed those retail traders with powerful tools recently available only to professionals working for Wall Street companies. Imposing "25K rule" on day traders changed the composition and numbers of retail traders; some changes in shorting rules, like abolishment of uptick rule, enabled traders with new capabilities while some other changes limited them. Simplification in order routing took away a certain edge from those who were proficient in that art, and enabled less sophisticated traders to obtain instant executions at decent prices. These and many other twists changed the industry in such profound ways and so rapidly, that the demands on adaptability became truly remarkable. The ability to adapt to such changes requires an open mind, sensitivity to changes and a careful probing of the new environment.

4. Self-effacing, like ice beginning to melt

Humility is one of the most important traits for a trader. This is his first and the most effective line of defense against market surprises. By being humble and remembering that the market is always stronger, he preserves himself from futile attempts to outsmart and out-stubborn the market. This is his protection against the arrogant stance of the 'I am right and the market must recognize it" kind. Knowing the market is capable of more surprises than he, the trader is able to foresee, he remains careful and alert. Remembering that he will never figure the market out in full, he remains ready for unforeseen turn of event. He never allows himself to relax and forget about inherent market risk.

A Taoist trader does not try to guess the moment of trend reversal. He realizes that such attempts would be akin to attempting to fight the market. He also understands that catching the exact reversal is earning him nothing but bragging rights – and this is not what he is interested in. Consistent and safe trading is not based on multiple guesses on the moment of a reversal, but on listening to the market and following its trend. Insisting on nailing the exact moment of reversal is an attempt to outguess the market; going with the trend until it changes is an admission of market superiority. A Taoist trader's philosophy is: **Letting the market tell you what happens next is humility; Thinking that you know better is arrogance.**

A humble trader sees no shame in going back to paper trading when he tries a new method. Nor has he a problem with small position sizes – it's an arrogant one who would consider it a shameful to trade on a smaller scale when circumstances are not conducive to excessive risk taking.

5. Genuine, like a piece of undressed wood

Many market patterns and characteristics are natural and intuitive – if we approach them without pre-conceived ideas and concepts imposed on us by various commentators. Take for instance the concept of euphoria and capitulation – very sharp rapid movements with big volume, defining the end of the trend and an upcoming reversal. Intuitively we tend to mistrust this kind of movements labeling them as "too far, too fast" – a familiar concept of a too large and rapid move being unsustainable. It is during such movements though that we are bombarded by upgrades, appeals to invest more and more, calling for higher and higher targets. Pundits for instance kept calling for new highs during the last days of the techno boom in 2000 – and even months after it peaked. Similarly, voices of doom and gloom called for exiting markets and staying away from them in March of 2009 when the huge rally started after the enormous and very fast drop – and continued calling to stay away or even short it for a year after.

If we manage to strip away layers of misconceptions and ideas imposed by propaganda, allowing our natural inner voice to be heard, we find answers to the many questions posed by the markets. These answers are intuitively understood; they are our natural reactions muted by those external layers creating a "crust" preventing us from being ourselves.

6. Open-minded, like a valley

We discussed open-mindedness in "**Grave, like one acting as guest**" as a necessary trait for adapting to changes. In all the examples we cited, one had to be flexible and capable of adopting new ideas – or he would have become obsolete in a course of months if not weeks. Such open-mindedness, willingness to accept change, adapt to new environment is a cumulative trait, consisting of many we discussed before – humility, preserving natural state, respect to one's surroundings.

Poem 76. Hard and Soft says:

When man is born, he is tender and weak;
At death, he is hard and stiff.
When the things and plants are alive, they are soft and supple;
When they are dead, they are brittle and dry.
Therefore hardness and stiffness are the companions of death,
And softness and gentleness are the companions of life.

7. And mixing freely, like murky water

A Taoist Trader accepts the market for what it is. He does not get angry at it, frustrated with it, elated by it. He never thinks of the market as being wrong or personally hostile. He does not complain about the market being impossible to trade or illogical. If he feels that way, he realizes that it's he who is out of tune with market. The Market is never logical or illogical, right or wrong, good or bad – it just is. For a Taoist trader, the market is his natural environment of which he is a natural part. He mixes with it freely and naturally, being comfortable but careful, reserved and respectful. Only by being a part of the market can he understand it, hear its messages, and be in tune with it.

16.
Knowing the Eternal Law

Attain the utmost in Passivity,
Hold firm to the basis of Quietude.
The myriad things take shape and rise to activity,
But I watch them fall back to their repose.
Like vegetation that luxuriantly grows
But returns to the root (soil) from which it springs.
To return to the root is Repose;
It is called going back to one's Destiny.
Going back to one's Destiny is to find the Eternal Law.
To know the Eternal Law is Enlightenment.
And not to know the Eternal Law
Is to court disaster.
He who knows the Eternal Law is tolerant;
Being tolerant, he is impartial;
Being impartial, he is kingly;
Being kingly, he is in accord with Nature;
Being in accord with Nature, he is in accord with Tao;
Being in accord with Tao, he is eternal,
And his whole life is preserved from harm

All the manifestations originate from a single source, the Tao. Manifestations can be observed and understood; Taoist philosophy is built on the foundation of these manifestations. This chapter introduces the concept of "chi" – the energy, or life-force, that unifies all mental, physical and metaphysical manifestations.

Chi permeates all living things. Not unlike blood through the arteries, chi flows along meridians in our body. Personal chi is improved by all things related to health – both physical (good food, exercise) and mental (a healthy mind, devoid of confusion and stress).

According to Taoist theory, at birth we carry pre-natal chi – the knowledge and experiences retained from all our previous existences. Then our intellect shapes our post-natal chi with the knowledge acquired through life experiences. Our ability to learn determines whether we pass life's tests.

Attain the utmost in Passivity,
Hold firm to the basis of Quietude.

*To "**attain the utmost in Passivity**" is a call for non-interference – Wu Wei, one of Taoism's cornerstone principles suggesting a Taoist to let things take their natural course and try not to change them. This next stanza speaks of the idea not to interfere with the natural rotation or cycles that exist in all phenomena:*

The myriad things take shape and rise to activity,
But I watch them fall back to their repose.
Like vegetation that luxuriantly grows
But returns to the root (soil) from which it springs.

*All "things" follow an unavoidable cycle of growth and decay during which they "**take shape and rise to activity**" and eventually "**fall back to their repose.**" This is true for people, plants, animals, even stars. Think of a perfect example: salmon returning to its cradle to complete the life cycle by giving the birth to the next generation and finding its grave. The poem declares that we "**watch them**" fall into repose, not interfering with their natural decline.*

To return to the root is Repose;

*"**Repose**" here references a state of peacefulness and calm. We reach this state by returning to our origins, or root.*

It is called going back to one's Destiny.

*"**Going back to Destiny**" sounds contradictive – destiny by definition lies in the future. The Taoist concept of time, however, is different from our traditional idea defined by clocks and calendars, where we move from moment to moment, day to day, always forward. For a Taoist, time is not linear but rather a spiral, or vortex. It is subject to the same cycles of reversion as all other natural expressions of the Tao. This concept is essential to understanding the idea of reincarnation as a second chance to rectify the mistakes of previous existences.*

Going back to one's Destiny is to find the Eternal Law.

The Eternal Law is Oneness – the unity of all Manifestations of Tao. Committing to the principles of Tao and going back to the natural laws, not those of society, an individual avoids confusion and sets on the path to contentment.

To know the Eternal Law is Enlightenment.

Enlightenment is a commitment to the Tao as a law governing all things, even though as limited beings we are unable to understand it in full. Such commitment requires a significant effort because seeing only a narrow slice of the vast system at work, to us the system sometimes seems chaotic and random. However, seeing how the universe continues to function, we must accept that it's our inability to rationalize its workings that makes the universe seem disorganized.

And not to know the Eternal Law
Is to court disaster.

*One of the biggest mistakes many make is rejecting the notion that we are limited in our ability to understand. Not being able to accept it, they try to fabricate a system of logic which makes them feel secure at the expense of shunning reality. Arrogantly trying to make the world conform to their ideals, they **"court disaster"** by acting on beliefs that contradict reality.*

He who knows the Eternal Law is tolerant
Being tolerant, he is impartial;
Being impartial, he is kingly;
Being kingly, he is in accord with Nature;
Being in accord with Nature, he is in accord with Tao;
Being in accord with Tao, he is eternal,
And his whole life is preserved from harm.

*Knowing that we cannot change anything beyond our own destiny, we are accepting of the Eternal Law. This neutrality and detachment places us **"in accord with Nature"** and causes us to avoid needless interference, conforming to the Tao and preventing us **"from harm."***

Attain the utmost in Passivity,
Hold firm to the basis of Quietude.

THE call for non-interference, while seemingly out of the realm of the retail trader who has little if any influence on the market, in reality is one of the most important concepts to adopt. Think of interference as an attempt to act against the natural forces and cycles, and the utmost importance of this idea becomes obvious. Passivity here does not mean doing nothing – it means allowing things to run their natural course and following that course instead of trying to oppose it. Counter-trend trading while the trend is strong would constitute such an attempt; so would overstaying one's welcome when the trend run its course. Understanding the cycles and patterns ("**Eternal Law**") allows a trader to find the course to follow it; such course is a path of the least resistance, or non-interference.

The myriad things take shape and rise to activity,
But I watch them fall back to their repose.
Like vegetation that luxuriantly grows
But returns to the root (soil) from which it springs.

Eternal cycles of growth and decay are true for the markets just as for anything else – which is only natural when you think of the market as one of Tao's manifestations and remember that market action is a by-product of people's action. Macro-trends form over the course of years and decades; micro-trends appear on a scale of weeks, days and even minutes. They obey the same laws and patterns – they "**take shape and rise**," and then "**fall back**" and "**return to the root**.'

Observing current events as they develop and analyzing historic events, a perceptive trader will detect in advance the repeated patterns of the cycle.

A trend usually starts slowly, almost reluctantly, easily unnoticed. Very few participants become aware of it at this point and join in. This stage is especially difficult to identify thanks to the absence of any good news, or even – in the case of a particular sector or a single company – news at all. Thus, movement continues for a while in a very quiet manner, carrying very few players on board. The next phase of the cycle can be characterized as "trend discovery" – more and more market participants start noticing that something is afoot. They join in, still in modest but increasing numbers. Their actions become almost a self-fulfilling prophecy as they attract more and more attention, thus drawing in more and more players. Not only price and volume action serves as an attractant, but also the media joins in, highlighting the events, publishing news, interviews and opinions. Finally, the notion of the market going up becomes "common knowledge" – everyone wants in, buy orders flood the market, the price spikes up on heavy volume as the last remaining fence-sitters pile on. The news flow becomes very loud and optimistic, commentators of all kinds promote the yet bigger gains to come – all the while the original buyers of the very first, quiet stage liquidate their position, selling into the hands of the eager latecomers. As the last arrivals bought all they wanted, there are no more buyers left, and the market has nowhere to go but down – thus the trend has exhausted itself and reversal time has come.

To return to the root is Repose;
It is called going back to one's Destiny.
Going back to one's Destiny is to find the Eternal Law.

Notice how the very beginning of the trend creates the foundation of its end in the future. Those same first buyers that initiated the move at its beginning, and those who joined them relatively early, are destined to become the sellers and effectively end the move. Today's buyers become tomorrow's sellers by the very fact of having an open position that will be liquidated at some point. Understanding this deceptively simple concept, a trader comprehends the idea of the market direction being defined not as much by news and other noise surrounding the market, but by the balance of potential buyers and sellers. Existing buyers are potential sellers – when they outnumber the potential buyers, "**going back to (their) Destiny**" they are going to tip the boat in the opposite direction. This is a situation called "overcrowded trade" in traders-speak.

As an extension of this same idea, by liquidating their long positions they free their monetary resources and become potential buyers once again ("**return to their root**") In other words, they are ready now to create the same cycle all over again – be it in another sector or company, in the same sector once the cycle is over or in the market in general.

The same logic of "overcrowded trade" obviously applies to the case of shorting. Too many existing short positions at some point create an imbalance. Being potential buyers as they need to close their position ("**return to their root**"), they will create buying pressure when they exit – sometimes fuelling sharp upward moves in what is known as a short squeeze. It's a reason for many traders to monitor the information about open short positions to spot potential imbalances.

To know the Eternal Law is Enlightenment.
And not to know the Eternal Law
Is to court disaster.

Understanding this cycle, learning to recognize it and discern its stages, arms a trader with the ability to position himself on the side of natural forces – take positions in the early stages of the move and liquidate them in the late ones. Imagine now the action of a trader who has no firm grasp of the natural laws governing the markets. He is likely to ignore first stage of the movement completely – simply because he places no significance in subtle price changes with no media buzz surrounding it. He is also likely to try and short the second stage of the movement, effectively "interfering" with natural market patterns – simply because the price movement, not supported by news and positive comments, is "not right" in his eyes. Finally, there is a good chance of him becoming a buyer at the last, third stage of the price advance – again, because in his view now that the media buzz surrounding the market becomes so positive he feels that the entry is justified. Therefore, we can see how absence of understanding of the patterns leads to confusion, focusing on the wrong aspects and eventually taking positions against the path of the least resistance ("**courting disaster**")

Another frequently seen example of erroneous behavior is a refusal to liquidate one's open position. Envision a trader who by chance took his long position at a good time – at the first or second stage of the upward movement. Lack of understanding the cycle pattern though prevents him from selling it when the market shows a parabolic spike. After all, the news is great and every pundit out there suggests buying. As a result, the trader misses the right time for exit, and then doesn't want to sell at the lower prices expecting market to bounce back. At some point his profits diminish to a level that makes no sense to take for him – and then turns into a loss. Every bull market has traders and investors that make fortunes on paper and give it all back by never exiting their positions.

He who knows the Eternal Law is tolerant
Being tolerant, he is impartial;
Being impartial, he is kingly;
Being kingly, he is in accord with Nature;
Being in accord with Nature, he is in accord with Tao;
Being in accord with Tao, he is eternal,
And his whole life is preserved from harm.

It's very helpful to see the analogy of the cycle described earlier in this chapter with many other natural phenomena. This cycle is not unlike a life sequence of a flower. Winter hibernation is followed by budding – quiet and unassuming process attracting no attention – unless you look for it purposefully. Opening of the petals is the next stage, finally followed by full bloom which attracts the most attention and represent the flower in its full glory. Of course, this is the end of the flower's cycle – just as full bloom and maximum attention signifies the end of the bull market. Change from the night darkness to first glimpses of the dawn to the moderate morning warmth to the glaring noon sun – and back to the evening chill illustrates the same daily cycle.

Moon phases, tides, rise and fall of cultures and civilizations – remembering that everything, being manifestations of the Tao, is a subject of the eternal ebb and flow, keeps us grounded and connected to reality. As far as the market is concerned, such an analogy helps us perceive its fluctuations as natural – and remain alert to recognize the signs of the different phases.

Such an analogy is also helpful to avoid assigning emotional labels to different stages. None of them are good or bad – they are all parts of the natural process. Similarly, no market participant or force is perceived by a Taoist trader as sinister or benevolent – he realizes that they all are market participants pursuing their own interests and his task is to decode their action instead of grading them on an ethical scale, which has nothing to do with reading the market action. This understanding helps preserve the emotional balance and detachment necessary for rational well thought-out action.

18.
The Decline of Tao

On the decline of the great Tao,
The doctrine of "humanity" and "justice" arose.
When knowledge and cleverness appeared,
Great hypocrisy followed in its wake.
When the six relationships no longer lived at peace,
There was (praise of) "kind parents" and "filial sons."
When a country fell into chaos and misrule,
There was (praise of) "loyal ministers."
That the credit cannot be taken away from him

The Decline of Tao describes how far artificial social values have moved us away from our original self-interest, natural instincts and personal contentment. Furthermore, it explains the power of the social structure in blinding us to the inconsistencies of society.

On the decline of the great Tao,

*The **"decline of the great Tao,"** while speaking of us losing our natural instincts, does not imply, contrary to some interpretations, that Taoism seeks a return to a mythical bucolic bliss, dismissing the comfort of modern civilization. Instead, the purpose of the Taoist philosophy is to help the individual maximize contentment within the conditions in which he lives. Referring to the "good old days" and lamenting that the Tao was in **"decline"** Lao Tzu explained that this fall is a part of the human condition. Our ability to reason and adjust is both a blessing and a curse. Engaging with society and interacting with its structures imposing their values on us, we tend to lose our natural instincts. Thus, **"decline of the great Tao"** is not a catastrophic one-time event– it's a permanent process taking place as societal values penetrate our state of mind and retreating as we progress on our way to enlightenment.*

The important ability of a natural state that is lost when we move away from it is the ability to live in the moment. While it may sound easy to accomplish, it is actually very hard to be fully engaged in each moment of life. Try to close your eyes and visualize a single image for one minute, while fencing off random thoughts, to appreciate the difficulty in controlling our scattered minds.

Living in a natural state forced man to be more engaged in the moment as the necessity demanded a more focused mind. Taoist philosophy helps us analyze priorities and the world around us, to see how external values influence our personal perceptions, thus helping us distinguish genuine motivations from those implanted by society.

The doctrine of "humanity" and "justice" arose.

*When Lao Tzu spoke of doctrines of "**Humanity**" and "**Justice,**" he referred to a value system reflected in the laws, customs, and traditions of the community. Individuals are taught to adhere to these rules to prosper (according to the society's definition), whether it makes them truly happy or not. Therefore, the social structure and peer pressure cause individuals to conform to the values of the system, ceding some control to the governing institutions.*

When knowledge and cleverness appeared,
Great hypocrisy followed in its wake.

*"**Knowledge and cleverness**" refers to the social value systems promoted by organs of communication designed to promote the needs of society. Hypocrisy can be routinely seen in social engineering throughout human history. Individuals portraying themselves as righteous defenders of ethical principles get caught in scandals, violating the very principles they championed. It happens regularly in all times and societies as self-interest causes the leaders and preachers to avoid the sacrifice they force upon others. Such hypocrisy exists on a larger scale beyond personal conduct, spreading to entire social layers. Their messages tell the individual that they exist to support him, as long as he adopts their recommended behavioral model.*

WE have discussed in previous chapters the purposes and mechanics of the upper echelon of investment community imposing certain ideas on individual traders and investors. This poem speaks to this theme once again. There are also other analogies helpful to a trader.

On the decline of the great Tao,

Deviation from natural state of mind, falling farther away from the right mindset is a frequent phenomenon among traders. Taught certain principles from childhood, then throughout our formal education and being bombarded with "axioms," even successful traders tend to relapse sometimes, losing that ideal approach that made them successful. Many traders encountered such situations described earlier in the chapter ***The Danger of Overweening Success.*** It is important to understand that as manifestations of the Tao, we are subject to its laws and patterns – and the pattern of losing our natural state of mind sometimes ("**decline of the Tao**") is one of them. It takes great humility and the power of detached observation to spot the moment when our mindset begins to deviate from the optimal.

A trader must realize that the mindset warranting successful trading is not instilled in us by our upbringing, in fact, just the opposite:

- We are taught to mold ourselves to the community and behave like everyone else, while successful trading requires detachment from the mass mindset and careful positioning against the masses when their ways become self-destructive;
- We are told not to time the market and invest in "professionals who know better," while performance of those "professionals" certainly proves that their timing is at least as bad if not worse during crises;

- We are told to "cost-average" during our investment life and not to worry about "short-term fluctuations," while those fluctuations are obviously capable of destroying one's chances for a comfortable retirement, especially when they happen near or during retirement! Those who invested in the stock market before 1929 didn't get even till late 1954, for example.
- We are subjected to the propaganda of banks and brokerage houses upgrading and downgrading certain companies, while statistics show that the timing of such coverage is far from optimal, and in many cases are outright harmful – just remember recommendations to buy Bear Stearns or Lehman Brothers days before their demise in 2008. (While on the subject, what better irony could you think of than Bear Stearns, an investment bank itself, being called the "Most Admired" securities firm in Fortune's "America's Most Admired Companies" survey in 2005-2007? Also, weren't these very institutions in existence from 1850 (Lehman Brothers) and 1923 (Bear Stearns), along with many others, the best illustration of once great entities losing their way following the pattern of the **"decline of Tao?"**);
- We are brought up to believe that the society will take care of us and guarantee us certain safety – belief that is sure to become our undoing in the markets where there is no safety net and nothing will prevent us from self-destruction should we act erroneously.
- We are told that paper loss is not a loss until we take it. Meanwhile, refusal to take a loss while it's small ties down our capital, severely limits our ability to act and weighs heavily on our psychological state – with possible outcome of never repairing itself in any reasonable time.

Reading through the list above you can clearly see the pattern in "who benefits" – that is, to whose benefit are all these rules designed to work. Most of them say "trust us with your money, we will take care of you" or "trust our recommendations, we know better what you need to do." Understanding this is not only important to start charting your own way in the markets. It's also very important to realize that being subjected to such massive propaganda at all levels and through all forms of communication, we have to work hard to keep the right mindset of self-reliance and critical thinking. As the propaganda itself adjusts, morphs and becomes more sophisticated, finding new ways and faces, the danger of falling victim is always there. The "**decline of the great Tao**" is always lurking around the corner.

The offer to invest into "great trading system that will produce profits without the need for you to do anything" is just another form of propaganda against Do-It-Yourself. So is the suggestion to pay for a "secret indicator that guarantees your trading success." So is "time-limited offer to subscribe to our great stock picks."

So, considering the need for education, how do you as a follower of Taoist principles determine who is a real educator worth your time and money? By using the same old Taoist principle we mentioned in previous chapters: a real mentor should be capable of applying his teaching in his own trading practices and succeed in the markets. One who can produce easy to verify proof of his trading abilities and consistent profits deserves your trust.

Returning to the matter of a trader's mindset deviating from the optimal, we need to address one more important aspect. What can we do to recognize such a deviation early and prevent it from causing sizeable loss?

At first, they're not easy to identify early. We simply have not enough experience to spot the early signs, and "fog of war" clouds our judgment. We need a formalized procedure allowing us to gain insight into our inner workings. The first step in such a procedure is recognizing the problem as it occurs. Our errors tend to repeat themselves over and over. In a while, it becomes obvious that a certain situation repeatedly provokes a certain response, and we get caught in the same trap time and again. One such example could be an attempt to buy each pause on the way down (short on the way up) in a vane attempt to catch exact reversals. Another frequent error is a massive overtrading after two or three losing trades, in the hope to repair the damage. Refusing to take a small stop, adding to a losing position – all those are harmful habits many traders find hard to break and tend to repeat them over and over again, even though most are aware of the destruction those habits cause.

One more important thing to keep in mind about these periodic relapses:, as a trader's experience grows they become less frequent and overcoming them becomes easier. At some point a trader masters the art of spotting them early and preventing them from developing so fully that they practically cease to be an issue. It becomes a matter of routine self-control that springs to action in certain situations almost automatically. Until it becomes a part of natural behavior, a trader must exercise purposeful conscious self-control.

Being in the moment is one of the most important characteristics for a successful trader. For a short term trader, it is necessary to focus on the action at hand not getting distracted by distant and irrelevant possibilities and information. Focusing on what's happening in front of his eyes, a trader is likely to see important signals as they are generated, instead of waiting for events that may or may not come in the future. He may have some target price for entry or exit in mind, but real time developments may alter his plans. Events occur here and now, and demand action as conditions change.

Longer term traders have a somewhat different definition of "being in the moment" as his reactions are not that immediate. However, the underlying principle is the same – filtering out the information in order to distinguish true signals from the noise generated by participants with agendas allows him to stay in a natural state of mind. An unclouded mind listening to the original market language maintains a magical mix of simplicity and sophistication.

There is another application of "being in the moment" in longer term trading. Oftentimes, a trader creates a certain model of events that he expects to unfold and prepares his actions accordingly. Actual developments meanwhile do not conform to that model. As a result, the trader stays on the sidelines at best or tries to act prematurely on his model not confirmed by reality.

In the best case scenario, he will miss a lot of other events before his model finally becomes validated by the market. Not only will plenty of opportunities be missed – when his scenario finally starts playing out, he is likely to be so upset by the long period of disconnection between reality and his model that he won't be able to fully trust himself and realize the full potential offered by market events.

In the worst case, the trader will try to jump the gun prematurely, insisting on his model being right and the market being wrong. Obviously such attempts will be punished severely causing significant losses.

The two best examples of such behavior could be seen in case of the great technological boom of 1998-2000 and the 13-months long rally started in March of 2009. In both cases, there were many traders insisting the market advance unjustified. Those who were patient enough to wait for the signs of the reversal had to wait for a much longer time than anyone realistically expected. As a result, they missed opportunities to profit from enormous movements. Had they stayed "in the moment" and traded what occurred before their very eyes, such opportunity would have been utilized, fully or partially. Those who had no patience and insisted on their model being right by trying to short both rallies were destroyed by the relentless market advance.

The doctrine of "humanity" and "justice" arose.

The social structure and peer pressure exists in the markets just as it does in every day life, and can be just as harmful for an individual. A trader absorbing volumes of information and views from various sources can easily become a follower of commentators whose priorities don't necessarily match his own. A trader participating in, say, online discussions can easily become a victim of "generally accepted" views. Imagine the pressure exerted by a group that unanimously agrees on a certain market direction or a certain stock pick. Our desire to fit in can be very treacherous, pushing us to agree, thus ceding control to someone else. It can be very difficult to maintain independence of thought under such pressure. It is, however, necessary to remember that commonly acknowledged views rarely if ever win in the market. Group thinking tends to be contagious – someone speaking with confidence and charisma can create a large following very quickly and become an acknowledged authority without producing any proof of his actual skills. A wise trader stays alert to any signs of group think forming and questions the premise or the leader, to make sure that the ideas advanced by the group are sound. If there are no easy to read signs either way, he will wait for the discussed developments to materialize so that he can evaluate the precision of the prognosis and scrutinize the group understanding.

When knowledge and cleverness appeared,
Great hypocrisy followed in its wake.

This again describes the pattern of a community interacting with the individual, subjugating him and making him a part of the crowd. A trader is promised to be taken care of if he follows the model suggested by this or that outfit or guru. "Follow our newsletter picks, signals generated by our system, investment advice by our experts and we will see that you are successful" is the message. No wonder that hypocrisy is frequently discovered in such interactions – the system designers do not trade it themselves; authors of the newsletter front-run their subscribers by taking position in advance and then selling to the subscribers and experts sell their advice never taking the recommended trades themselves. Even track records are sometimes falsified by using many clever tricks.

Again, a trader is well advised to use his common sense to verify the validity of claims. Armed with a deep understanding of a proven approach, an experienced trader can often evaluate the soundness of the philosophy applied by this or that guru or outfit by simply comparing it to what he knows is working. A newer trader must observe actual performance before making conclusions, even though claims sound very convincing.

20.
The World and I

Banish learning, and vexations end.
Between "Ah!" and "Ough!"
How much difference is there?
Between "good" and "evil"
How much difference is there?"
That which men fear
Is indeed to be feared;
But, alas, distant yet is the dawn (of awakening)!
The people of the world are merry-making,
As if partaking of the sacrificial feasts,
As if mounting the terrace in spring;
I alone am mild, like one unemployed,
Like a new-born babe that cannot yet smile,
Unattached, like one without a home.
The people of the world have enough and to spare,
But I am like one left out,
My heart must be that of a fool,
Being muddled, nebulous!
The vulgar are knowing, luminous;
I alone am dull, confused.
The vulgar are clever, self-assured;
I alone, depressed.
Patient as the sea,
Adrift, seemingly aimless.
The people of the world all have a purpose;
I alone appear stubborn and uncouth.
I alone differ from the other people,
And value drawing sustenance from the Mother.

Contrasting conflicting goals of society versus the individual, this poem identifies the characteristics that Taoist should possess and explores the pressures applied by communities on individuals. It also reminds us that the attributes of a Taoist are viewed through society's eyes as undesirable.

Banish learning, and vexations end.

*"**Learning**" here refers to the knowledge and belief system put forth by the society and propagated via various means of communication. "**Vexation**" results from the corrosive nature of artificial and irresolute value systems.*

How much difference is there?
Between "good" and "evil"

*Definitions of "**good**" and "**evil**" and resulting laws and customs differ from society to society and from one time period to another. Such arbitrary changes of laws throughout every country's history, or the differences between countries at any point in time illustrate the profound difference between Nature's principals and man-made rules. As discussed earlier, following the natural laws and patterns results in the individual's contentment while applying artificial values leads to confusion and aggravation.*

That which men fear
Is indeed to be feared;
But, alas, distant yet is the dawn (of awakening)!

Societies coerce desired behavior punishing and embarrassing transgressors. Instilling fear in the common man, they ensure conformity and subordination. There is, however, another reason why the Taoist has reservations about social structures.

As witnessed in each country at any time, the difference between personal expectations and reality results in doubt, confusion and anxiety in men's minds. Yet society routinely promotes values that can cause trouble for the individual when questioned. While insisting that the state guarantee safety and comfort of the individual, while promoting the sacrifice of self-interest in the name of the common good, societal value systems aim to preserve societal structures, not the individual. This is a very important point: since society puts a premium on compliance, its prescribed behavior is not likely to bring personal contentment. Designed for self-preservation, social institutions promote interests that can be harmful to an individual's contentment.

This point explains the Taoist's fears. Being a member of society however, he needs to find the way to enjoy his life and not wield a fruitless fight against societal institutions – respect the Tao of Man (the social structure), but live by the Tao of God (Nature's principles).

The people of the world are merry-making,
As if partaking of the sacrificial feasts,
As if mounting the terrace in spring;

*"**Merry-making,**" "**sacrificial feasts**" and "**mounting the terrace**" are references to the many social conventions attractive to the common man. The Taoist understands that many are happy with these superficial recreations and should be left to their preferred activities.*

I alone am mild, like one unemployed,
Like a new-born babe that cannot yet smile,

This stanza speaks of the Taoist's relatively lonely way of life among the vast majority who do not share his views. Practicing a philosophy that questions conventional values and institutions, the Taoist must be ready for such outcome. The ***"new-born babe"*** *is a reference to being unpolluted by the external values. Not being taught what to value as good or bad, the newborn* ***"cannot yet smile"*** *and its reactions are natural and untainted.*

Unattached, like one without a home.

The Taoist; values bring him contentment whether the social structure approves of them or not, thus he is "unattached." Instead of accepting community dogmas that can vary with time and place, he embraces absolute principles.

The people of the world have enough and to spare,

This line speaks of the people who have adequate resources to enjoy their lives, yet continue to acquire more and more. Time lost and opportunities squandered can not be bought back with an excess of riches accumulated beyond what is necessary.

But I am like one left out,
My heart must be that of a fool,
Being muddled, nebulous!
The vulgar are knowing, luminous;
I alone am dull, confused.
The vulgar are clever, self-assured;
I alone, depressed.
Patient as the sea,
Adrift, seemingly aimless.

The Taoist does not share the quest of common men. He works for personal contentment, not for the luster of commonly accepted signs of success, even though it may make him appear as a "fool." Those who share generally accepted values feel ***"knowing, luminous, confident and clever,"*** *not realizing the emptiness of their pursuits. The Taoist may seem* ***"dull and confused,"*** *his life* ***"aimless and adrift"*** *to them as his values are far removed from theirs.*

The people of the world all have a purpose;
I alone appear stubborn and uncouth.
I alone differ from the other people,
And value drawing sustenance from the Mother.

This stanza, as a whole poem, speaks of Taoists ***"differing from the other people."*** *The majority of people* ***"have a purpose"*** *defined by the society, which they unquestioningly follow. The Taoist, following eternal principles, marches to his own beat.*

CONTRASTING conflicting goals of established market institutions versus the individual trader, this poem identifies the characteristics that a Taoist trader should possess. It also highlights the fact that the attributes and views of a successful Taoist trader are likely to be viewed by many with hostility.

Banish learning, and vexations end.

In a perfect analogy with Taoist principles, "**learning**" here refers to the knowledge and belief system promoted by the multiple institutions creating the noise surrounding the markets and propagated via various means of communication. It's not an accident that many successful traders speak of turning down the TV, refusing to read popular market overviews or newsletters. Focusing on pure market action instead of listening to the views dictated by agendas frees them from the influence of external sources and guarantees objective perception of the events. Others review such sources of information skeptically and scornfully, almost for entertainment value alone. Third and the most sophisticated group keeps listening and reading those sources to be aware of agendas promoted, to evaluate whether crowds get enticed by it and to spot the moment when the market action sets the trap for those overly trustful. "**Vexation**" inevitably results from the non-critical acceptance of popular views.

How much difference is there?
Between "good" and "evil"

Many erroneous ways to deal with market reality stem from stubborn and dogmatic attempts to assign 'right" and wrong" labels to various actions. There are endless examples of such simplistic one-dimensional approaches. Unsophisticated commentators and traders expect the price to drop on any bad news and advance on good news. Opposite price action is being labeled as "wrong" and called manipulation. Not only does such an approach dismiss one of the major market characteristics we discussed earlier – acting against the obvious, punishing those who try to trade with what everyone knows and rewarding those who understand that those are losing ways – but this way of thinking also causes much aggravation, instills constant anger and most importantly – firmly puts a trader on the losing side. It's hard to think of a less productive position than one that causes resentment against the very nature of the market.

Such a position also ignores the real subject a trader must focus on: price action. A Taoist Trader realizes that price changes can occur with no material news, and often becomes a self-fueling development. One needs go no further than the infamous Procter & Gamble 50% price cut followed by an almost full rebound in a matter of minutes on May 6, 2010. Even though that particular price movement was attributed to an alleged computer glitch, it contributed greatly to the market's enormous intraday move (990+ points Dow Industrials) impacting many other stocks. Extreme as this example is, you will find similar events on a lesser scale almost daily – price changes not caused by simplistic news influence, occurring for unknown and unknowable reasons and happening against straightforward logic.

Another frequently observed error is expectation that the market should act according to one's ethical principles. A trader projecting his views of good and bad on the market expects the price to reflect such views. Needless to say, there are many market factors in play that have little if anything to do with ethics. To cite a few glaring examples of irrelevant views on the market:

- shorting tobacco company stocks because smoking is a bad habit;
- shorting oil-related company stocks because they pollute and use up the non-renewable resources;
- shorting gun manufacturer stocks because guns are evil;
- buying alternative energy company stocks because they produce clean energy and use renewable sources.

While any of these directions may be and often are profitable, such trading decisions should not be made on ethics based grounds. In most cases, very different reasons cause price change, and most of them have nothing to do with "good" or "bad." Now, if an investor refuses to put his capital in stocks of the companies whose products contradict his moral views because he doesn't want to support them – it's a perfectly acceptable approach; it, however, is different than expecting the price to follow one's morals.

One more often seen example of imposing moral views on the market action is an attitude toward shorting. Sometimes labeled as an anti-patriotic activity, shorting is viewed by some as harmful and unethical, as "betting on failure." In reality of course it's nothing of the sort – it's simply recognition of the natural patterns we discussed earlier, particularly in Chapter 16 ***Knowing the Eternal Law.*** Such mistaken attitudes toward shorting also ignores the fact that shorting provides the balance to price action and softens future declines, since every short position holder is a future buyer. It's important to understand from where such hostile perception of the shorting comes. The majority of individual traders and, especially, investors prefer and understand the long side. It's also a part of the propaganda by money managing machines – "in the long run the market always goes up." Those who do not conform are viewed with hostility; those who take opposite positions are viewed as causing harm; those who profit from the movement that causes the majority's losses are viewed as enemies. There are many historical and contemporary examples of this attitude. Jesse Livermore received death threats after profiting by shorting market crash of 1930; Senate hearings in 2010 revealed great contempt for "betting against housing market."

That which men fear
Is indeed to be feared;
But, alas, distant yet is the dawn (of awakening)!

All entities and structures surrounding the market are motivated by their own interests. Their interests are not aligned with those of individual traders. Promoting their own agenda, they need obedient followers, not independent thinkers. There is a good reason why many downgrades occur after the sizeable move down and upgrades – after the substantial move up.

Offering their guidance and services, many institutions advance views that serve their interests first. A wise trader knows that his personal success is not found in submission to the commonly accepted outlook.

The people of the world are merry-making,
As if partaking of the sacrificial feasts,
As if mounting the terrace in spring;

A Taoist Trader also knows that he needs to find a way to follow his own understanding of the market without trying to fight those organizations. Such attempts are futile – they find a large grateful audience that willingly accepts their advice and will vigorously defend their idols. There is no point in trying to re-condition those who are only too happy to follow their gurus; a wise trader may offer his views and leave it to the listeners to accept or reject them.

I alone am mild, like one unemployed,
Like a new-born babe that cannot yet smile,
Unattached, like one without a home.

A Taoist trader knows that many of his views will put him on a lonely path. This is perfectly acceptable for him and serves as a confirmation that he is taking the right position. In fact, he will worry if he finds himself siding with the majority of those discussing market events and likely direction. Knowing that the majority is unlikely to be correct, he will pause, step back and re-evaluate his stance. Like a "**new-born**," his mind is unpolluted by conventional beliefs and his reactions are in tune with natural laws of the market.

The people of the world have enough and to spare,
But I am like one left out,
My heart must be that of a fool,
Being muddled, nebulous!
The vulgar are knowing, luminous;
I alone am dull, confused.
The vulgar are clever, self-assured;
I alone, depressed.
Patient as the sea,
Adrift, seemingly aimless.
The people of the world all have a purpose;
I alone appear stubborn and uncouth.
I alone differ from the other people,
And value drawing sustenance from the Mother.

The interesting phenomenon a wise trader is bound to notice is a loudly expressed confidence by those who subscribe to commonly accepted views, or stubbornly insist on their being right. It's much more common for a really knowledgeable experienced trader to sound reluctant, to be unsure of the future developments and admit it openly. Knowing how uncertain the market is, he is not so quick to express full confidence; he accepts that events may develop in unforeseen way, and such acceptance makes him better prepared for an unexpected turn of events. A Taoist Trader's plans and prognosis are usually tentative, with provisions for various conditions. They will include many "ifs" and "buts." He would rather plan for multiple scenarios than put his full confidence in a single one.

This is where many Taoist concepts discussed earlier come together in a wholesome mindset. Let's try and piece some of it together:

A Taoist Trader recognizes that the knowledge possible to gather is limited, thus he needs to accept the uncertainty in which he operates –this gives him both humility and decisiveness. Humility keeps him safe – he applies strict risk control to protect himself from the unforeseen turn of event. Decisiveness comes from strict discipline – knowing that he is protected by his risk control measures he does not hesitate to act. It may sound paradoxical, but in fact, lack of confidence about his ability to foresee market events gives him confidence in his actions.

A Taoist Trader recognizes that forming a firm opinion about the market direction is likely to trigger intervention by his ego and make him stubborn in the event he is wrong. It also can make him elated in the case of being right. Both emotional states will impact his objectiveness, distort his perception and take away the focus of detached observer. Thus, he follows the market indications, accepting any possible outcome in advance and not locking himself into any opinion. Such a mindset puts him beyond right or wrong and leaves him free to follow the market's current. He simply acts when he encounters a recognizable situation for which he has a pre-canned response. In a way, his trading becomes quite machine-like. Having no opinion to defend, he has no ego to protect and no emotional investment to shield.

Such an approach makes him ever the oddball in any discussion about market events. While everyone around expresses an opinion and expects him to do the same, he sounds unsure and can offer little in a sense of predictions ("**adrift and aimless**") Many good traders are well known for their 'I don't know" answer when asked about what the future holds – unlike market commentators who make a living by talking and not by trading, and usually have many "predictions" to offer. Real trader's forecasts often irritate the audience because they contain many conditions and reservations.

This mindset has profound influence on one's stance in life, well beyond trading. Such an attitude is in fact life-altering, as it suggests a whole new way of looking at the world, at the events, at the people around you, and relationships with them. Learning to trade is a process of learning and changing oneself, and such change is bound to affect one's attitude toward the world around him. It's not really a surprise when you think what's involved: a trader must understand how the masses feel and think, yet be capable of detaching himself, staying unaffected by mass emotions and common thinking. The enormity of such an undertaking is hard to overestimate. It's also not a surprise when you think of the laws that govern the market. Those are the same laws that govern nature, psychology and the world. When you establish this connection you harmonize yourself with the market, making your trading effortless and profits natural. At the same time, instituting such harmony you make trading a natural part of your life that comes in balance with any other. It doesn't become the only passion eating a disproportionally large portion of your time. It doesn't make you unhappy – it allows you to live in peace and accord with yourself and those close to you. While it may sound trivial, it's not – many struggle to incorporate trading in their life in a harmonious way.

22.
Futility of Contention

To yield is to be preserved whole.
To be bent is to become straight.
To be hollow is to be filled.
To be tattered is to be renewed.
To be in want is to possess.
To have plenty is to be confused.
Therefore, the sage embraces the One,
And becomes the model of the world.
He does not reveal himself,
and is therefore luminous.
He does not justify himself,
And is therefore far-famed.
He does not boast of himself,
and therefore people give him credit.
He does not pride himself,
and is therefore the chief among men.
It is because he does not contend
That no one in the world can contend against him.
Is it not indeed true, as the ancients say,
"To yield is to be preserved whole?"
Thus he is preserved and the world does him homage.

This chapter discusses how contention wastes time and energy, detracting from achieving the goal.

To yield is to be preserved whole.

Knowing when to stop ("yield") is a critical warning in Taoist philosophy. "Never enough" causes one to pass by happiness in the constant chase for more. For the Taoist, to have enough is a blessing while attempts to acquire beyond the necessary leads to contention and wasteful competition.

To be bent is to become straight.

Taoism's governing principles differ from those held by public. They appear "bent" to the masses. Knowing how little tolerance there is for unconventional ways of life and how his indifference can be viewed as confrontational, a Taoist remains careful not to display his thoughts, values and beliefs to the close-minded around him.

Because the social structure is so enormous and pervasive, we must interact with it constantly. Trying to change it is futile and would consume too much energy. Nature, as another large structure, coaches us to accommodate and not challenge its power. Animals do not try to alter the ruthless realities of the jungle – instead, they routinely adapt to their environment and react to situations. They appreciate their limitations and don't try to extinguish forest fires or antagonize larger predators. They have no problem running from danger. In a similar sense we should accept our weaknesses.

To be hollow is to be filled.

Our community's value system comes complete with a set of recommended desires and expectations for happiness and success – unobtainable for some, unsuitable for others. While Taoists are subject to the same social pressures as everyone else, they strive to rid themselves of unattainable desires and expectations. When this line urges us "to be hollow," it suggests that we rid ourselves of artificial values, while becoming "filled" with the values of the Tao.

To be tattered is to be renewed.

Lao Tzu cautions the individual to "never be first in the world." It is a warning to never stand out from the masses, thus avoid contention. When we try to prove that we are better than others, the result is usually resentment or anger. Jealousy makes you a target. The poem stresses the usefulness of being useless ("tattered"), as someone demonstrably very good at something will be a target for those who will want to exploit his skills.

To be in want is to possess.

As in Buddhism, Taoists see the human suffering rooted in their desires. We suffer because of spiritual or material desires that we cannot satisfy. However unlike the Buddhist philosophy, Taoists do not seek to fully rid themselves of physical, mental, or emotional desires. Instead they strive to recognize their individual limitations to accomplish what can be accomplished, and restrain that which cannot.

To have plenty is to be confused.

To have enough, is to have the means for contentment, and avoid the entrapments of "never enough" – a societal value which keeps us in competition with others as there will always be someone who has more.

Therefore, the sage embraces the One,
And becomes the model of the world.

The Taoist embraces the Tao – the source of all things ("the One" in this stanza). Within Taoism there is a set of governing principles according to which the natural world operates. Embracing these principles, the Sage becomes a micro-version of the larger natural system and thus "becomes the model of the world."

He does not reveal himself,
and is therefore luminous.
He does not justify himself,
And is therefore far-famed.
He does not boast of himself,
and therefore people give him credit.

Understanding that the world lives by another set of values, the sage avoids conflict with the social structure whenever possible. He is content in his beliefs and has no need to justify his values to others. An unassuming life keeps him free of unnecessary conflicts.

He does not pride himself,
and is therefore the chief among men.

Taoism considers pride a harmful trait. It separate the individual from the Tao, antagonizes the people around him, shows his arrogance and provokes anger. Instead, the Taoist maintains humility and keeps his pride in check. Taoists believe that they have no right to judge other ways of life. The lessons of Tao are so deep that even a lifetime of study may provide only a basic understanding – so there is no room for pride.

It is because he does not contend
That no one in the world can contend against him.

Because the Taoist quietly goes his own, there is no noticeable difference between him and his neighbors. He remains focused on doing what is necessary and leaves others alone, not interfering with their way of life. This does not mean there will not be conflicts, for peace will be disrupted by clashes. But without inviting contention, "no one in the world can contend against him."

Is it not indeed true, as the ancients say,
"To yield is to be preserved whole?"
Thus he is preserved and the world does him homage.

Taoism works because it teaches us how to follow our beliefs while effectively navigating everyday life. The social structure is much stronger than any single person and one must respect its strength, while following one's own path.

THE very title of this poem for an experienced trader immediately invokes associations with correct behavior in the markets. Mantras "don't fight the tape," "market is always right," "trend is your friend" are all saying the same thing. Just as contention with social structure in Taoist philosophy, contention with overwhelming market forces is futile and harmful.

To yield is to be preserved whole.

This line is a very succinct yet very precise reminder about use of stop loss as a method to preserve one's trading capital. To yield to the market force that moves against one's position is to save avoid the much greater problems later (**Deal with the difficult while yet it is easy; Deal with the big while yet it is small.**While a beginning trader will hesitate to take a stop thinking of it as a loss, he allows a loss to grow and stays tied down with no capital for better trades, a Taoist Trader knows that a timely taken stop preserves his financial standing and keeps him capable of engaging once again at a better time.

To be bent is to become straight.

Many traders encountered a situation where a social interaction would go sour as they merely answered a question about their profession. In the eyes of the many, trading is an unproductive and parasitic profession. As Taoist principles look foreign and unacceptable to the masses, so can the profession of trading – and just as a Taoist, a trader may prefer to camouflage so as not to invite irritation and hostility.

The market environment, as a society, is not to be changed. Its vast structure contains many elements and interactions – some of them may look unfair or unseemly to us. Many spend their time and effort complaining about real or imaginary violations, manipulations and unethical behavior. Browsing the Internet, you may stumble onto numerous forums and blogs fully devoted to angry discussions of anything perceived as "wrong" with the market – sometimes reflecting actual problem, oftentimes showing nothing but a lack of knowledge of market mechanisms. A Taoist trader knows that various abuses have occurred throughout the history of the market; fighting each and every one of them is a waste of time. The market structure is very complex, and for an ordinary observer it's not always possible to distinguish real abuse from a totally valid transaction. A wise trader will consider such tilting at windmills as an unproductive waste of time, preferring to study market mechanisms and find inefficiencies to exploit.

To be hollow is to be filled.

There are many false beliefs imposed by the market environment on an individual trader. We listed some of them in ***The Decline of Tao***. Similarly, "right" methods of trading are promoted and pushed under the disguise of wisdom, of non-arguable truth. Let's list some of those pseudo-wise maxims of which a trader better stay "hollow to be filled."

- Sell in May and go away *(much good would it do for a trader in 2009 – and that's not an isolated example).*
- Buy a stock in a company whose product you like and would use personally *(give it 3 minutes of thought remembering different companies that did well and thinking of their products to quickly see that most of them you would never be able or want to use for your personal consumption).*

- You can't go broke taking profits *(Of course you can – if you take smaller and more frequent profits than you do losses).*
- Buy low, sell high *(Works nicely in a ranging market, but makes you buy against the market in a downtrend and short against it in an uptrend).*
- As goes January, so goes the year *(If only trading were that easy! Why don't we see financial institutions taking position according to January's result, leaving them for the rest of the year – and making money?)*
- As goes the first week of January, so goes the month, and so goes the year *(Better yet – one week must be enough to make the right financial decision for the whole year?).*

To be tattered is to be renewed.

Lao Tzu's caution to "never be first in the world" is often a perfect strategy in the markets. When you are looking for a reversal during a stock's fall, it's rarely a good idea to step up and be the first buyer. A much wiser approach is to wait for a stock to start showing strength – which obviously will be the result of other traders stepping up. The same can be said about exiting at the top and attempt to short there. While missing an exact low or exact top doesn't sound very glamorous, it guarantees that your entry will occur in a much safer situation with better odds of working out.

Another example of "not being first" is an entry for a breakout while facing a large amount of shares at the break level. Instead of initiating his position and waiting to see if others join in, a wise trader will wait for that resistance to melt down and only then enter.

To be in want is to possess.
To have plenty is to be confused.

The insatiable desire to chase the unobtainable, thus causing suffering, is a perfect metaphor for a trader holding his position beyond a reasonable price target. Every movement in the market is good as long as we can read it. A trader should close his position when his system signals that the move is over. Of course any situation may resolve in an even bigger move, but this is where a wise trader draws the line. He takes profit when he can't read the market anymore. Holding his position beyond such a moment is pure gambling and wishful thinking. More often than not it will lead to evaporating profits.

Of course if a further move after the position is closed occurs regularly, a trader needs to review his exit criteria. Such an approach will be a wise adjustment to changing conditions, an improvement upon his current skills and tools.

Therefore, the sage embraces the One,
And becomes the model of the world.

The idea of a micro-version of the larger natural system ("**becomes a model of the world**") reflects in a few aspects of trading.

One is the fractal nature of the market. It's important to realize that most patterns occur in different time frames and work in a very similar fashion. You can observe a trend on yearly chart, daily chart or intraday 1 minute chart, and if you cover the time scale, there will be practically no way to tell which is which. When you study a certain chart formation, trading setup, repeated pattern you usually can safely apply it to any other time frame. It can be useful in cases where you stumble onto interesting trading setups described by the author for a different time frame from the one in which you operate. If you, for instance, see an article written by a day trader and like a chart formation he uses for his trades, it's very likely that you will find the same formation on a longer time frame chart and will be able to utilize it.

Another application of the concept "**the sage... becomes a model of the world**" lies in the idea of using your own emotional perception to understand the emotions driving the trading masses. Harmful emotions that plague a beginning trader's actions are the same across the board. Learning to suppress them and eliminate them from your trading decisions, you don't eliminate emotions themselves – you only dull them and separate them from your actions. However you still can observe them in a cold-blooded detached manner. Using them as a mirror, you turn them into a window for understanding how crowds act. That panic you can feel in yourself observing a steep sell-off is what drives scared traders to hit "sell at market" buttons. The temptation to buy during sharp vertical spike is what lures in future bag holders. Having developed chart reading skills and learning to use your emotions in such a way, you gain an ability to stay on the right side of the market.

He does not reveal himself,
and is therefore luminous.
He does not justify himself,
And is therefore far-famed.
He does not boast of himself,
and therefore people give him credit.

Many traders waste a lot of time trying to convince others that their views and opinions about the market direction or particular position are right. Countless hours are spent online in arguing about future events, sometimes those that will be revealed the very next day. Such arguments are absolutely pointless and serve no useful purposes. If for some reason you have a need to share your trades, post them and let future events speak for themselves. There is no need in justifying your decisions, recruiting the like-minded or convincing opponents. Not only will it bring nothing but the aggravation of unavoidable conflict, it will also make you close-minded as you get locked in your expressed opinion. If you need to voice a certain point of view, make sure that you make it conditional, depending on certain developments – this way you preserve flexibility of thinking and leave yourself room for adjustment as new information comes in. It will also be of more benefit to your audience (at least to those who want to learn), as they can understand your way of thinking and not just see the final conclusion.

He does not pride himself,
and is therefore the chief among men.

Pride in trading is just as dangerous a trait as in all other aspects of life. Desire to earn cheap bragging rights pushes a trader to try and catch exact tops or bottoms – and such attempts are harmful to his trading account. Taking a loss may feel like wounding one's pride and push him to refuse to take a stop, eventually leading to a much larger loss. Bragging about good trading performance makes us feel as if we have to maintain our image and keep our results just as excellent all the time. That again distorts our perception of market reality and creates unneeded pressure. It's necessary to remember that we all are just students of the market – the learning process never ends as the market constantly presents new challenges. No one possesses a monopoly on the ultimate truth. Humility keeps us grounded, our emotions in check and our trades – rooted in reality.

It is because he does not contend
That no one in the world can contend against him.

This stanza is another reminder about necessity to stay in tune with market rather than fight it. Massive market force breaks the obstacles appearing in its way – a Taoist Trader knows not to be an obstacle.

24. The Dregs and Tumors of Virtue

He who stands on tiptoe does not stand (firm);
He who strains his strides does not walk (well);
He who reveals himself is not luminous;
He who justifies himself is not far-famed;
He who boasts of himself is not given credit;
He who prides himself is not chief among men.
These in the eyes of Tao
Are called "the dregs and tumors of Virtue,"
Which are things of disgust.
Therefore the man of Tao spurns them.

This poem is closely connected to the previous, ***Futility of Contention****, and reminds us about the duality of all the manifestations. Virtue, as everything in the world composed of opposites, contains both positive and negative (****"dregs and tumors."****) Virtues in eyes of society turn out to be harmful to individual contentment. Social virtues often demand sacrifice from the individual. Taoism distinguishes between socially defined "virtues" used for control vs. those used for personal freedom. Chuang Tzu addresses this issue in his essay "'He Who Reveals Himself is not Luminous.' The Definition of Good."*

What I call good at hearing is not hearing others but hearing oneself (the individual). What I call good at vision is not seeing others but seeing oneself. For a man who sees not himself but others, or takes possession not of himself but of others, possessing only what others possess and possessing not his own self, does what pleases others instead of pleasing his own nature.

He who stands on tiptoe does not stand (firm);
He who strains his strides does not walk (well);

Standing on tiptoe and straining one's stride refers to unnaturalness, causing discomfort in standing and walking. Unnatural behavior not based on healthy self-interest takes away from a content existence.

In the essay quoted above, Chuang Tzu recommends "taking good care of one's character" and "fulfilling the instincts of life." Caring for one's character means formulating a clear picture of the world and your place in it.

Emotion is an inherent and necessary component of our nature. It can also be the basis of our greatest delusions. Our ego leads us to believe that we are rational beings in control of our emotions. In reality, the opposite is true. We have the capacity to be rational, but emotions can often direct our decision-making. Taking control of our emotional side requires a dispassionate analysis of our life, formulating a firm philosophical foundation of our outlook and creating rational routines to govern our actions.

He who reveals himself is not luminous;
He who justifies himself is not far-famed;
He who boasts of himself is not given credit;
He who prides himself is not chief among men.

Maintaining the Taoist principle of contrasting opposites to illustrate the point, this stanza describes the characteristics of a person not living by the virtues of a Taoist as described in **Futility of Contention.** *Such an individual does not understand his place in the world. He competes with others by boasting, therefore attracting contention. He is stressed by the unnecessary pursuits and overburdened by his pride leading him to belittle those around him. All these qualities in the eyes of Tao are* **things of disgust***.*

AS social virtues often demand sacrifice from the individual, it can happen sometimes in the markets as well. We mentioned earlier an example of presenting shorting as anti-patriotic activity, demanding that a trader refrain from it for "moral" reason even though such activity can and often is quite profitable; widely used by institutional market players, it serves a useful purpose. We also mentioned a suggestion to abstain from buying stocks of companies whose product may not sit well with certain ideologies or views popular at the moment – gun manufacturers, tobacco companies, oil producers. Let's add to this array another case: appeal for "socially responsible investing." This is a perfect case of market structures suggesting something that can be quite harmful for a trader's performance under the pretense of "doing the right thing." Buy the shares of clean energy related companies (solar, wind, tide etc.), and you are doing your share of good for the planet. Needless to say, when looking into such purchases, a trader would be well advised to analyze the odds of a stock performing well – his purpose is to make money in the market, not to contribute to unknown companies, people running them and banks selling public offerings. There is nothing unethical in refusing to invest in such companies blindly, based solely on the fact that they work in a certain field. After all, if they run their business well enough to achieve their noble purposes, it will be reflected in their stock performance and a trader will react on signals from the chart. Buying the stock to donate to a good cause and suffering a loss because of the poor management of the company in question is not going to help the cause. A Taoist trader will do his homework when hearing such a call; his "whose interest it is for" radar will go up when told that he should do the right thing by buying into certain company.

Chuang Tzu's essay "'He Who Reveals Himself is not Luminous.' The Definition of Good." Certainly rings a bell for a trader's mindset.

What I call good at hearing is not hearing others but hearing oneself (the individual). What I call good at vision is not seeing others but seeing oneself. For a man who sees not himself but others, or takes possession not of himself but of others, possessing only what others possess and possessing not his own self, does what pleases others instead of pleasing his own nature.

No trader ever built a sound approach and successful trading career on listening to someone's tips, entering and exiting positions based on someone's opinions and taking information from the outside without critical analysis. Be it a friend, a relative, a co-worker, some on-line or TV personality, there are many concerns about taking their word on faith and acting on it. Obvious problems with this are:

- you never know whether there is an agenda behind their advice;
- you rarely know their level of qualification;
- even if you have all the reasons to trust their honesty and skill, their risk tolerance, time horizon and expectations are likely to differ from yours;
- following their advice you do not develop your own approach and stay dependent on their "charity."

Those are not small concerns that can be easily overcome. Instead of doing their own research, such traders continue asking the 'tip givers" what they think; they don't know whether those sold already or are still holding their positions. They may be told that the losing position is being kept for prolonged period of time while they had no such intention; or that the position was sold already at prices no longer available, and they have no way to know in time to do that or if that is even true. This approach leads to anxiety and dependency.

He who stands on tiptoe does not stand (firm);
He who strains his strides does not walk (well);

One of the frequent errors associated with this stanza is lack of trust in one's own system and method of reading. Even if testing shows consistent solid performance, a trader acts as if he has no faith in it and exits his positions prematurely, not letting his system play out as it should. Profits taken as soon as they appear, no matter how small they are is a frequent symptom of this problem. Doing this, a trader practically chokes his performance, not allowing himself to extract any serious money from the market. Fear to let any profit go robs him of a worthy profit. Even worse, this behavior is often combined with blowing one's stops. This combination leads to profits being much smaller than losses – an arrangement destructive for a trading account.

Fear of a loss can also make a trader take the loss before his actual stop level is hit. This leads to trading on noise – insignificant, almost accidental movements that do not signify any meaningful chart signal. Naturally, trading on random movements produces random results. The combination of taking smallish losses and profits with no chart indication for either is not much better – it produces a lot of commissions and meaningless trading account churn. Even if no significant losses result, expenses and commissions bleed the trading account while his sound trading system remains idle.

The reason for this irrational behavior is of course our emotions. The emotional side takes over and controls our decision-making process to a much greater degree than we are willing to give it credit. We like to think that we can rein our fears and hopes and act on pure rationale. In reality, it's possible only with immense work and effort aimed at nurturing self-control and discipline.

Taking control over emotions involves several steps.

First, relatively easy and most obvious is the realization how exactly emotions in trading harm our performance. We discussed in earlier chapters how the way trading masses act is exactly the wrong way to act. It is emotions that govern their actions – and if we allow emotions to govern ours, we are going to join the crowd in its self-destructive behavior. Armed with this understanding, we realize that we need to isolate ourselves from this powerful influence so we can detach ourselves from the crowd.

Our next step is devising a sound healthy philosophical system describing our understanding of the markets, our place in them and the model of our behavior in the market. This step is what you are doing at this moment studying the application of Taoism to trading.

Finally, third and the most difficult step is practical implementation – actual dealing with our emotional side, taking back control over our own actions. This is done by designing and implementing a set of routines – templates for our action in various circumstances. First we need to create a list of standard situations we encounter in our trading. Such a list will include trade initiation, exiting on the loss side, exiting on the profitable side, taking partial profits, trailing stops. It also is likely to include certain circumstances where we need to refrain from taking the position – market movements creating the temptation for impulsive entries (quick seemingly unstoppable spikes so enticing to chase, quick sizeable price drops creating the impression that a bounce is imminent) or losses causing the desire for revenge trading. For each standardized situation we need to create a routine describing our response. New templates can be added as we encounter and diagnose certain psychological problems which damage our performance.

This set of routines creates a matrix of our behavior in the market. Combined, they provide us with detailed step-by-step instructions describing what to do when certain situations are encountered. These standardized instructions give us clarity, chip away at uncertainty, and add confidence in our pursuit of emotional control. This effect decreases psychological pressure and allows us to diminish the impact of emotions on our trading.

Another aspect of trading where we observe a positive influence from having standardized, established templates is recognition of certain market situations that call for a standard response. It can be a particular trading setup or more general situation shaping up in a big picture market – having a standard situation resembling it in your arsenal and knowing how it's likely to develop gives you an enormous advantage, as we discussed in the chapter 15. ***The Wise Ones of Old***.

Let's cite an example of one of such routines to illustrate their use.

Revenge trading.

This situation is a frequently seen one. A trader encounters a loss at the start of the day (we are talking about a day trader here simply to compact the experience in a short time frame; it will be done along similar lines for any other time frame). Not willing to accept the loss, he starts pushing hard for remediation, initiating trades where there is no valid setup for them, digging the hole deeper and, again, pushing harder. As a result, the day ends with a sizeable loss, much bigger than the initial one that caused the spiral of self-destructive behavior.

According to our steps above, let's go over them one by one. First step: Diagnosing the problem – we just did it in the paragraph above. Some particular details added to such diagnostics can be an exact number of losing trades or dollar amount of a loss that triggers the harmful behavior. For the purpose of this exercise, let's say it's a $200 loss. Second step is creating a solid philosophical foundation. In this particular case, a Taoist trader realizes that his knowledge is limited – as a manifestation of Tao, he can not know all there is to know. He can not predict the future, thus there is always room for an unforeseen turn of events. It means that losses are unavoidable and a certain percentage of losing trades are expected. The cyclical nature of all phenomena also means that winning trades will take turns with losing ones. Losses in such a view become a normal, natural, and inalienable part of the trading process. Thus, there is no need to be alarmed by it and try to eliminate those losses or take immediate revenge.

With this in mind, let's design a **Revenge Trading Prevention** routine.

Routine trigger: loss of $200.

Reaction:

1. Leave your computer for 30 minutes. Go outside, do a breathing exercise. Recite the part of your trading philosophy describing the place and role of losses in trading (in order to make this part more standardized and effective, you may come up in advance with a mantra on the subject to recite).

2. Return to your computer. Start observing market action trying to view it as a fresh start, as if your day just started.

3. Your next three trades are going to be paper trades. Pay special attention to the reason for the trade – make sure that your entries are based on real setups, not on wishful thinking. Staying with paper trading will give you back your discipline – discipline of stopping yourself from harmful behavior, taking back control over your action.

4. If your trades continue losing, stay with paper trading till the end of the day. If they are winning ones, start trading real money again but with half of your usual position size.

5. When you establish firm pattern of returning to setup-based trading as opposed to emotion-based trading right after returning to your computer, you may switch back to real trading skipping paper trading stage, but with half lot position size.

All the steps described above will stop you from repeating the pattern of self-destructive behavior, help you bring up the inner discipline and turn you into calm detached trader with highly developed self-control.

You will find more examples of routines in an attachment at the end of this book.

He who reveals himself is not luminous;
He who justifies himself is not far-famed;
He who boasts of himself is not given credit;
He who prides himself is not chief among men.

This stanza describes the characteristics of a person not living by the virtues of a Taoist as described in ***Futility of Contention*** (possessing qualities that are **things of disgust**). There is great practical use for this contrast for a Taoist Trader. Just as you create a model of a great wise trader for you to become, create a model of a confused trader acting as a part of the crowd. Now and then, compare yourself to that model to see whether you inadvertently preserve some of their habits or exhibit some of their behavior. It will help you move farther from self-destructive behavior and mold yourself more precisely into what you consider a model trader. Approach this with the same thoroughness as the creation of your ideal. Think through all the traits and actions of the hapless traders. What is it they do in this or that situation? Do they fail to apply proper stops? Chase parabolic moves, buy near the top? Try to go against the current, jumping in on a sharp move down before any sign of bottoming appears? Average down increasing their risk? As you go over such actions and qualify them as **things of disgust**, you increasingly know what not to do.

29.
Warning Against Interference

There are those who will conquer the world
And make of it (what they conceive or desire).
I see that they will not succeed.
(For) the world is God's own vessel
It cannot be made (by human interference).
He who makes it spoils it.
He who holds it loses it.
For: Some things go forward,
Some things follow behind;
Some blow hot,
And some blow cold;
Some are strong,
And some are weak;
Some may break,
And some may fall.
Hence the Sage eschews excess,
eschews extravagance,
eschews pride.

This poem concentrates on one of the most important principles in Taoism: Wu Wei. Often mistranslated as "action/inaction," its true meaning is "non-interference." Wu Wei instructs us to not take action unless something interferes with our pursuit of contentment; to not interfere with others unless their actions interfere with ours. It is also a warning to not interfere with our own nature. ***You could describe Wu Wei as the right action, in the right time. The right action in the wrong time is still wrong. The wrong action at the right time, produces the same result.***

The Tao Te Ching instructs the ruler to govern in a laissez-faire way. For the individual, the principle similarly advises us to harmonize our existence with the Universe, not interfering with the natural forces governing all existence.

There are those who will conquer the world
And make of it (what they conceive or desire).
I see that they will not succeed.

*Nothing lasts forever. Attempts to **"conquer the world,"** and **"make of it"** something envisioned by the conqueror **"will not succeed."** because the very process of forming an artificial structure is an exercise in constraining natural forces, which is to plant the seeds of future downfall.*

(For) the world is God's own Vessel
It cannot be made (by human interference).
He who makes it spoils it.

*The scale of the Universe and the principles that govern it are well beyond our capacity to comprehend. When we try to change or enhance **"God's own Vessel,"** our actions are likely to contradict those principles, thus interfere. Therefore, these actions are destined to fail (**"spoil it."**)*

He who holds it loses it.

*If the process of keeping one's cherished possession requires force, then it is interference. By interfering with the nature of a phenomenon you degrade it, thus hastening its failure, and you **"lose it."***

For: Some things go forward,
Some things follow behind;
Some blow hot,
And some blow cold;
Some are strong,
And some are weak;
Some may break,
And some may fall.

Everything has individual characteristics and, at the same time is governed by the Principle of Reversion. All manifestations undergo a cycle of growth and decay; no amount of interfering can change that reality.

Hence the Sage eschews excess,
eschews extravagance,
eschews pride.

***"Excess"** is going beyond what is necessary (**"Never too much"**). Going beyond natural limits, requires more effort than necessity dictates. Therefore excess is interference since it violates the natural harmony of the system.*

***"Extravagance"** is unrestrained overindulgence that violates Lao Tzu's advice "Never be first in the world." By being extravagant, not only do you spend disproportionate time and effort, but you are probably doing it in a way that makes you exceedingly visible, attracting conflict.*

*"**Pride**" is one of most hazardous traits. It distorts our view of the world and removes us from reality. Since Taoism is about seeing Ultimate Reality, an exaggerated view of our abilities and self-worth makes it impossible to follow a path towards contentment.*

WU Wei, "non-interference," is one of the most important principles in trading. We have touched on its trading applications before. Let's recall the aspects of this concept as they apply to trading.

The most crucial way in which Wu Wei reveals itself in trading philosophy is a warning to not interfere with natural market trends. Trading in the trend direction is effortless – the market grants you profits by simply taking you with its current. Attempts to fight the trend lead to multiple losses or, if you get stubborn, one devastating loss.

Another frequently seen violation of this principle is intrusion in the normal development of the open trade. As your open position dances up and down not resolving into hitting your stop loss or achieving profit targets, such movements are nothing but noise. Until meaningful price levels are broken, this noise doesn't tell anything about the way a trade is going to resolve. Your stop and target must be located in a way that factors in those noteworthy price levels; thus, any action taken before they are achieved is interference with normal processes.

The Tao Te Ching instructs the trader to harmonize his actions with the market, not interfering with its natural forces that govern all price changes.

There are those who will conquer the world
And make of it (what they conceive or desire).
I see that they will not succeed.

Just as the process of forming an artificial structure is an attempt to constrain natural forces, so is a process of forming an opinion about future market direction and sticking to it despite the market behavior saying otherwise. This type of conduct can be seen in most communities discussing the market practically all the time. Let's describe it in detail so you can recognize it when you encounter it in others, or see it in yourself. In the process, we are also going to tie it up with several other principles we learned from the Tao Te Ching. If you have been a participant in almost any on-line forum devoted to market events, you no doubt will recognize the development described below.

Based on certain assumptions and analysis of the economy in general or state of the particular industry or company, an individual or a group arrives at a certain conclusion about the future market direction which is supposed to reflect their conclusion. Observing such a discussion, you can often see an overstated confidence in their analysis expressed loudly and buoyantly. This over-emphasized self-assuredness is your first warning signal as it goes against several Taoist principles we learned earlier. To list them:

- arrogance in not recognizing that our knowledge is limited, thus our conclusions are not guaranteed to be correct;
- justifying the decisions and arguing with others, thus reinforcing emotional commitment to an expressed opinion and losing flexibility of the mind;

- getting passionate and emotional about the conclusions and related market positions, thus losing objectivity.

If the next price movement goes against the estimation made by the group, you will often see exultation. In a paradoxical way, holders of the opinion convince themselves that such a move confirms their belief. Their logic usually is: the market shakes out weak hands; this adverse move is a head-fake, the last shakeout before turning in their favor. Often-used phrases at this stage are: "They are not getting my shares cheap," "They are not going to fool me," "They are not shaking me out," "I can see through their games" etc., along these lines. Their jubilance is often expressed in an idea very familiar to any participants of such discussions: "This latest price move is an excellent opportunity to add to our position at even better prices." You may see triumphant exclamations like "Thank you market makers!" or seemingly reasonable self-reassurances such as "If I liked this stock at $20, I like it even more at $15." Being armed with sound Taoist principles, you can easily see everything that is wrong with this: arrogance, denial of the possibility of being mistaken, pride, and confidence in their model as the only right one.

As the market continues moving against the original judgment, participants of the discussion face rising losses. This is the moment when their confidence is really put to test. Instead of taking the loss while it's small and re-evaluating their opinion, they normally continue their stubborn ways. As a student of Taoism, you understand why: their Ego has sprung into action, triggered by opinions expressed publicly and loudly. They now have more than just money on the line – they have reputations to protect and pride to save. Admission of fault is not an option – it would hurt too much, for some even more than the monetary loss. As time goes on, their loss becomes unbearably large, to the point of total destruction of their trading capital. At this point they need to find something or someone to blame for their defeat and come up with the next step.

As far as blame assigning goes, the traditional foe chosen for this purpose is "market manipulators" – whoever they might be. It's manipulators' intrusion in the market cited as the reason for the market moving against what seemed so obvious. Looking into the validity of this claim, it's easy to see from the point of view of the Taoist Trader that it's simply irrelevant – whether manipulation takes place or not, it has to be included in the trader's view of the market as one of the moving forces. The trader's objective is to determine the direction of the market and to take the correct position. To do so, he must account for all forces involved in price change. While reference to manipulation might be a valid explanation for the movement that takes place, it is unforgivable for a realistic trading approach to ignore such a possibility and stubbornly fight against it.

As for the next step, this is where a Taoist Trader will also act very differently from most participants of such discussions. Locked in their opinion and angered by apparently being wrong, they usually get enraged, express bitter disappointment with the market and proclaim self-removal from the trading process. Some of them take enormous losses; some decide to stay with their position in hope the market comes back in the future. You can see them continue to argue those same points as they did in the beginning of the debacle, explaining to anyone willing to listen that they were right all along and that sinister market manipulators destroyed them. All kinds of conspiracy theories arise, invoking scorching hot negative emotions. No reasonable voice is getting through as they do not want to hear the truth – all they want is justification for their action. Needless to say, a Taoist Trader, knowing that his model of the market can and often will be wrong, allowing for reality to be different from what he envisions, staying humble and striving for clarity in seeing what really happens, will cut his losses well before they become so painfully large. Realizing that job number one is to stay in tune with the market and get a sense of the trend, he will spot the divergence between obvious information and price action. Understanding how the action along the lines of the obvious becomes a trap for the masses, he will take the opposite position, thus aligning himself with the natural forces of the market. Possessing the powerful weapon described in Chapter 24 ***The Dregs and Tumors of Virtue*** (comparing his behavior to self-destructive models), he will spot the group's erroneous conduct early and avoid aligning himself with their action.

(For) the world is God's own Vessel
It cannot be made (by human interference).
He who makes it spoils it.

One application of this stanza is obvious and mentioned earlier; let's deepen it and make the next step in practical application. Our job as traders is to observe and discern the market's natural patterns and align our behavior with those patterns. We can't impose our ideas on the market and expect it to work according to our ideas – rather we have to come up with ways to exploit patterns existing in the market. This concept goes to the heart of any trading system – setups that govern our action.

Not knowing how to go about designing such setups, some traders simply come up with some assumption as they try to make trades based on it. You can spot this approach by seeing them applying arbitrary price levels for entering their orders while not being able to demonstrate any statistically valid pattern confirming their method and working over a long time. Their explanation will often be limited to references to "sensing," "feeling" or at best showing a few examples from recent charts. Obviously such an approach usually doesn't work other than by accident. This is a typical example of "***who makes it spoils it.***"

Instead, the sound approach based in observing and recognizing reality is constructing the setups coming from the market itself. Be it chart patterns or certain technical indicators, your setups must fulfill certain requirements to be a solid foundation of your trading approach. Let's list such requirements so that you can verify any of those you come up with against this list.

1. The setup must make sense from the point of view of the trading philosophy. By trading philosophy we of course mean Taoism applied to the market. If we are looking at the breakout setup for instance, we want to apply a concept of water breaking the dam as we discussed in the Chapter 8 ***Water.*** If it's a trend reversal setup, it should go along the lines of the Chapter 2 **The Rise of Relative Opposites,** Chapter 16 **Knowing the Eternal Law** etc. All the elements of the setup must be presented in accordance with Taoist principles; we will give related references as we go over them.

2. The setup must make sense from the point of view of trading psychology. Understanding how masses think and act and realizing that their trading decisions are usually wrong, a Taoist Trader makes sure that his setups incorporate this concept. Each element of the setup must be verified from the point of view of "what not to do" – which is what masses normally would be doing. He knows that trading masses tend to chase vertical price spikes and are usually left holding the bag. Thus his setup must prevent him from entering on such a spike. He also knows that crowds tend to fight the trend by arbitrarily entering long positions during downward moves or short ones during upward moves. Thus he will avoid taking such positions without clear indications of a trend reversal.

3. The setup must clearly identify an entry point – trigger for initiating the trade. While a trading philosophy gives a general idea of such triggers (breakouts, reversal formations etc.), particular parameters must be confirmed by the observations of the price action, both in the past and presently, in different types of markets. If we are looking for a breakout setup, we need to go over charts showing the formation that we intend to use and compare those that worked in the past with those that failed, to come up with a clear idea of what we want to see for the successful breakout. For instance, looking at the Cup and Handle (one of the typical breakout chart formations), we will want to know:
    - **3.1** How does the volume shape up for the confirmation of the successful break?
    - **3.2** How long the Cup should take to form?
    - **3.3** How long the Handle should take to form?
    - **3.4** Is there an optimal ratio for those time parameters?
    - **3.5** How deep the Cup should be?
    - **3.6** How deep the Handle should be?
    - **3.7** Is there optimal ratio for those price parameters?
    - **3.8** How should the broad market act to support or invalidate the breakout?

    Looking at the Double Bottom (one of the typical trend reversal chart formations), we will ask a similar set of questions: volume confirmation, relation between price levels of both bottoms and the peak between them, market directional support etc. Analyzing past performance, we come up with an idea what works and what doesn't for a successful setup, thus designing our trading system. Finally, in terms of the trigger for the trade we look for the "decisive moment" – action that signifies the setup taking place. There could be many variations for that; normally for the breakout setup, break of the resistance formed by a consolidation range (rim of Cup and Handle for instance) serves as a trigger, while for a trend reversal setup the trigger is a break of resistance formed during a bounce attempt (peak between two bottoms for Double Bottom setup). A trader may choose to enter before or after the actual trigger of course – those are variations of a particular trading system. The system itself, however, must include the precise description of the setup with all its elements.

4. The setup must clearly identify stop loss point. Such a point is defined as the sign that the original idea of the trade is not valid anymore. It comes naturally from the setup itself and has its roots in the concept that we are not able to predict the future with full certainty. Limited in our abilities to grasp the scope of the complex system in which we operate, we must make sure that our losses are minimal in those cases when we are proven wrong (stop it while it's small). Thus, when we analyze a breakout setup, we determine the sign of a breakout not working in our favor. For that same Cup and Handle, the sign is the price moving below the Handle's bottom because that is the support level which indicates failure if broken. Similarly, price moving under the level created by two bottoms indicates a failure of the reversal.

5. The setup must instruct us about the exit point on the profit side. Closing the position must be based on the same philosophy we discussed earlier – doing the opposite of what the trading masses tend to do. Let's recall the idea that the majority tends to chase vertical price spikes and is usually left holding the bag. Thus our setup will include a full or partial exit when such a spike occurs favoring the direction of our open position.

He who holds it loses it.

Interfering with the phenomenon's nature by "**holding it**" has three applications in trading.

One has been discussed extensively earlier – stubborn insistence on being right, continuing to do what hasn't worked. Aside from being stubborn in any particular trade as it proves to be a losing one, this trait tends to manifest itself also in persistent repetition of the same manner of trading – even as it shows no profit and leads to consistent losses. This is behavior that can be observed time and again as traders continue doing the same thing that is obviously and demonstrably the wrong thing to do. Seeing that it doesn't work, they promise themselves that they won't do it anymore, only to repeat the same behavioral pattern the next day. This unrelenting behavior seems to be something out of their control, as if some external force takes over and makes them do it repeatedly, against their own better judgment. A Taoist Trader knows that this conduct is caused by emotions taking over and making us act irrationally. His way to prevent such ruinous action is to design and apply routines governing his reactions and keeping him strictly disciplined, as described in Chapter 24 ***The Dregs and Tumors of Virtue***.

Another way in which "**holding it**" applies to trading and leads to "**losing it**" is holding open positions for too long, thus allowing them the reverse and profits – evaporate. It is remarkable how even getting the idea of the trade right and initiating a timely winning position still can, and often does, result in losses if no timely exit is deployed. Any big market move is packed with stories of such occurrences. The Tech boom of 1998-2000 brought fortunes to many, only to see those riches slipping away and turn into devastating losses as traders kept their position well beyond the peak. A similar story arose in the oil price explosion with price reaching

$150 in the summer of 2008 only to drop back to under $40 – all the while experts predicted it going higher and higher. There is nothing new about such behavior either – the well know tulip mania of the 17th century, the South Sea Bubble – in 18th; it is obvious that such mass behavior is generally typical for human beings. Sure enough, being a philosophy for the individual, Taoism arms a trader with the arsenal necessary to avoid becoming a victim of this destructive conduct. Knowing that things develop in cycles and the fall inevitable follows the rise, understanding the "never too much" principle, learning to avoid excesses and being perceptive to recognize the excess in mass behavior, a Taoist Trader will be on the lookout for the signs of decay slowly shaping up under the sparkling surface of the seemingly unstoppable rise. Knowing how over-confidence often signifies mistaken stance, he will be careful not to align himself with the masses that are overly assured in a never-ending trend – witness the housing bubble of 2002 – 2007.

Finally, the third way in which this stanza manifests itself is in the manner of many traders trying to over-exploit the pattern that slowly ceases to work. Just as anything else, market patterns go through cycles of performing brilliantly, then decaying slowly, ceasing to work altogether and finally being re-born and blooming once again. A Taoist Trader will stay sensitive to these changes, adjusting as his setups change performance.

For: Some things go forward,
Some things follow behind;
Some blow hot,
And some blow cold;
Some are strong,
And some are weak;
Some may break,
And some may fall.

This stanza reminds us once again about eternal cycle of growth and decay that governs all phenomena. There are some important applications for a trader in this list.

While broad market movement usually influences most stocks and sectors, this influence is not spread out evenly. There are constant changes to the flow of leaders (***things*** that ***go forward***) and followers (***things*** that ***follow behind***). Some sectors and stocks move first, others follow them with a certain delay. These relations can be spotted and exploited to a trader's advantage. If there is a pattern of such following that can be observed regularly, it gives a clear trading idea. Seeing a leader stock moving, a trader can use the delay to initiate a position in the follower stock. It is important to remember that most of these relations are fluid – they tend to work for a while, then change or disappear altogether.

It is paramount for a trader to follow the activity. Some sectors become more active now and then (**blow hot**) and some become very inept (**blow cold**). You can sometimes see traders continuing to follow familiar names long after they become inactive; they do not pay close attention to the natural dynamics of the markets and try to squeeze something out of a stock or sector that became dormant.

Whether it's a desire to stay in a comfort zone of familiar companies or simply lack of awareness, it keeps a trader focused in the wrong area.

There are also natural relations between various sectors. A Taoist Trader keeps watching such relations and tries to stay on top of the changes. To demonstrate an example of such relationships and their transformation, let's look at the triad of oil, airlines and the general market in 2008 – 2009. As oil prices soared, airline stocks got pounded – the logic in traders' mind dictated hardship for the airlines during sky-high fuel prices. This inverse relation between oil and airline stocks existed for a few months; then as oil started its rapid retreat, airline stocks somewhat recovered. As time went, however, other concerns took over – the broader economic crisis started influencing the airline sector as travel and shipment volumes decreased. This same crisis greatly diminished the demand for oil. As a result, general market direction started governing the oil price – new logic dictated that improvement, or lack thereof in the economy impacted the demand for oil. By the same token, the state of the economy impacted the demand for airline services. Thus, new relationships established – both oil and airlines started following the general market, losing the inverse relationship between them.

As we can see, these relationships are fluid. Their logic is not always easy to foresee. As everything in the markets, we can come up with certain assumptions but eventually it is up to the market to confirm or invalidate our scenario. Changes in relationships between the US dollar and gold is constant evidence of how non-obvious these balances can be. At some times gold obviously works as a hedge against a weakening dollar, establishing the inverse relationship. Both, however, went up when crisis in Europe widened in 2010 threatening the monetary union and Euro as a currency – traders obviously viewed both the US dollar and gold as a safe haven in their flight from Euro, thus ruining the inverse relationship between them.

Hence the Sage eschews excess,
eschews extravagance,
eschews pride.

This stanza returns us to the concepts we have discussed before. Use this chance to re-read the explanations below and think of the trading applications we have talked about earlier, refreshing them in memory and seeing them from new angles.

"**Excess**" is going beyond what is necessary, beyond natural limits offered by the market movement. Therefore excess is interference since it violates the natural harmony of the system.

"**Extravagance**" is lack of moderation that violates Taoist advice "Never be first in the world." By being extravagant, a trader spends disproportionate time and effort in pursuit of the unnecessary.

"**Pride**" is one of the most hazardous traits. It distorts a trader's view of the market and removes him from reality.

37. World Peace

The Tao never does,
Yet through it everything is done.
If princes and dukes can keep the Tao,
The world will of its own accord be reformed.
When reformed and rising to action,
Let it be restrained by the Nameless pristine simplicity.
The Nameless pristine simplicity
Is stripped of desire (for contention).
By stripping of desire quiescence is achieved,
And the world arrives at peace of its own accord.

"Wu Wei" is often explained with confusing citations such as "Do nothing, and all things will be done," or "Tao does not act, yet there is nothing it does not do." These quotations frequently lead to the erroneous conclusion that the Tao Te Ching recommends we need not do anything, letting life take care of itself. It of course makes little sense in the real world.

"Non-interference" suggests the individual must prudently choose either to act or not act. Contentment means being at peace. To be at peace one must accept his personal strengths and weaknesses. To control emotions, which motivate interference, one must achieve a state of calmness. In his essay, Doctrine of Inaction and Quietude, Chuang Tzu wrote:

"The sage is calm not because he says to himself, 'It is good to be calm,' and therefore chooses to be so. He is naturally calm because nothing in the world can disturb his mind.... non-interference means being at peace with oneself, and when one is at peace with oneself, sorrows and fears cannot disturb him..."

To practice non-interference with one's original nature, one must remove society's interfering influences by sticking to a comfortable daily routine. This routine reinforces one's self-control and calmness by simple repetition.

Wu Wei has a number of other implications for personal peace through non-interference:

First, the duality of opposites in any phenomenon entails that we will go through alternating periods of relative happiness and sadness; times of success and times of failures. To expect otherwise is to believe we can interfere with the natural cycle of life. Therefore, our emotions should reflect this awareness by neither being too jubilant when things are good nor too disconsolate in times of trouble. This attitude leads to the desired state of calmness.

Second, according to Wu Wei, by not interfering, energy is conserved so that there's ample stored power available when necessary. Like a coiled spring whose energy is stored until released when called upon, we need to preserve energy to be prepared to act when the situation requires. Chang Tzu wrote: "He responds only when moved, acts only when urged, and rises to action only when he is compelled to do so."

The Tao never does,
Yet through it everything is done.

*The Tao goes about its business, driven by the principles of Nature. There is no consciousness to its actions, so it "**never does.**" But the principles operate as they always have, and "**everything is done**" as it has always been.*

"Not doing" in terms of the Tao Te Ching terms not only recommends non- interference, but also refers to the skill with which Wu Wei is applied. When the individual has internalized Wu Wei, no conscious thought is involved in the application, it should be automatic.

If princes and dukes can keep the Tao,
the world will of its own accord be reformed.

*"**Princes and dukes**" are the rulers who attempt to control their subjects. If they relinquished their artificial values and adopted Taoist standards, the people and relationships would eventually return to their original nature ("**be reformed.**") This Taoist society would not be a Utopia – it, however, would operate consistent with Nature's way, including conflict, predators, and their prey.*

When reformed and rising to action,
Let it be restrained by the Nameless pristine simplicity.

*Once people adopt the principles of Taoism, "**rising to action**" fulfills their original nature, the "**Nameless pristine simplicity**" – their original simplicity uncorrupted by artificial values.*

The Nameless pristine simplicity
Is stripped of desire (for contention).
By stripping of desire quiescence is achieved,
And the world arrives at peace of its own accord.

*Desires are normally dictated by the values adopted by the individual. To find one's true nature, artificial social values must be stripped away. Stripping away the "**desire for contention**" is an instruction to avoid the implanted need to compete for the unnecessary trappings of success. Actions motivated by one's original nature remain in accord with one's nature and lead to natural harmony.*

STATE of calmness is one of the most important parts of a trader's mindset. It's crucial for ensuring an ability to make decisions in cold blood, unclouded by emotions. It is in a calm relaxed state that a trader is capable of choosing his action in accordance with objective, observable indications and not under the influence of his needs, wants and emotions. A trader must be at peace with himself and the market as his environment. To remove fear from the decision-making process, a trader must accept his limitations and act within those limits. This approach will keep him in familiar territory with which he is comfortable. To remove the unwarranted hopes, a trader must understand his place and role in the markets. This will keep him grounded and realistic. It doesn't mean he should not strive for more but it's important to realize that increased profits can and must be earned through acquiring new knowledge and improving his skills. Each can obtain what he deserves in the market. This "deserving" has nothing to do with fairness or ethics. It is understanding the market laws and acting in accordance with them with steel discipline that makes one worthy of reward in trading and opens the possibility for making profits.

Just as the sage from the Chuang Tzu essay, a Taoist Trader is naturally calm because he is at peace with himself and understands his surroundings.

Maintaining a calm, balanced, state of mind requires insulating oneself from the aggravation of the incessant flow of the news and comments by all kinds of market, economic and politic pundits. It is easy to observe how close listening to this flow and taking it to heart makes one constantly exasperated. It's important to remember that news agencies have their interests and agenda – it is the sensational and the horrific that attracts the audience and helps raise the ratings. Objective balanced reporting takes a backstage – and so does the informational value of the media. Such skewed reporting makes a sincere listener feel infuriated by all the wrongs of the world. Understanding the nature of such reporting, careful choice of sources and filtering the information is a Taoist Trader's trait.

The concept of using a daily routine to maintain a calm state of mind is perfectly applicable for a trader. We already spoke in Chapter 24. ***The Dregs and Tumors of Virtue*** about using routines designed for specific situations to minimize the influence of emotions. In the same way, a general daily routine keeps a trader in his comfort zone and gives him a calm balanced state of mind. Such a routine includes his morning actions – firing up the software, checking the overnight news developments, and evaluating the state of the market. It continues with forming his working assumptions for the market action and choosing his reactions. Further, typical market changes depending on the time of day and various scenarios are included in a trader's routine and he observes the events to determine which of the scenarios takes place, thus electing the requisite response. It is highly recommended for a trader to include meditation in his routine. We include some meditation techniques in the attachment at the end of this book. Those go a long way in putting a Taoist Trader in the balanced state of mind and keeping him calm, relaxed and ready for action.

Other implications of Wu Wei for a trader's personal peace:

First, the duality of opposites necessitates that we will go through alternating times of success (profitable trading) and times of failures (losing trading). To expect otherwise is to believe that we are above the natural cycle of life. Therefore, it is important to keep emotions in check in both parts of the cycle – not get too elated during success and not fall in despair during failure. This attitude will lead to calmness.

As a side comment to the concept of going through natural cycles of profits and losses:

- If you hear someone claiming to have no losing trades, you know you're dealing with deception.
- Limiting your losses by applying stops is crucial for your survival as a trader
- Going through prolonged periods of successful trading, instead of becoming reckless try to apply an extra-careful attitude to stay sensitive to the signs of market change, so as to not get caught off guard when the cycle reverses.
- Going though prolonged periods of losses, cut down your aggressiveness and position size to minimize losses and stay sensitive to signs of market change to be ready to engage more actively when the cycle reverses.

Second, applying the Wu Wei principle of conserving energy, learn to stay inactive when the market is not teeming with opportunities. We need to preserve attention and capital to be fully deployed when the situation is most advantageous. If the market stalls during lunch time for a day trader, he needs to cut down his activity. The market may become less active seasonally (summer time overall and August especially) – trader's aggressiveness must be adjusted accordingly. Wasting time, occupying one's mind and tying up capital in unproductive trades lessens our preparedness for better opportunities.

The Tao never does,
Yet through it everything is done.

The market goes about its business just as the Tao does, driven by the principles of Nature, without consciousness to its actions. "**Everything is done**" simply by the markets natural action. It's important to understand these natural ways of the market to remain objective and not to personalize the interaction with the market. The market is not after you personally, nor is it hostile to you – although not friendly either. If certain situations feel like someone out there watches your actions to immediately move the price against you – all it tells you is that your actions are not aligned with the market trends.

"**Not doing**" in trading, as in the Tao Te Ching, also references the skill which makes good trading effortless. Observing a successful trader operate, you will often see that his actions are almost automatic, as if no conscious thought is involved. You will also hear comments that "he makes it look easy" – this is one of the true signs of high level skill.

If princes and dukes can keep the Tao,
the world will of its own accord be reformed.

This stanza in trading terms refers to the authorities trying to interfere with market actions through various methods of intervention and constant tweaking of the rules. If they left the market alone, they would allow the market to perform its major function – price discovery – much more efficiently ("**be reformed**")Of course, it doesn't mean that the market would have become a Utopia – it, however, would operate consistent with Nature's way, with natural conflict, predators, and the prey. This doesn't mean that the market subjected to intervention by authorities and overzealous regulators becomes of no use to a trader. Just as a Taoist finds the way to practice his beliefs in the world ruled by the societal structures, a Taoist Trader accounts for such interventions in his market reading. In other words, interventionists become another factor for him to consider; their tracks become another footprint to read, and their intentions – another variable to observe.

When reformed and rising to action,
Let it be restrained by the Nameless pristine simplicity.
The Nameless pristine simplicity
Is stripped of desire (for contention).
By stripping of desire quiescence is achieved,
And the world arrives at peace of its own accord.

Once interventions in the market cease, it quickly restores its natural ways and returns to the price levels reflecting the reality as market participants understand it. Its actions become uncorrupted by the authorities' interests and start reflecting actual supply and demand. It is also important to understand that no intervention can keep the market in an unnatural state forever – the longer interference continues the steeper the eventual reaction is. Artificially limiting volatility will eventually resolve into extremely violent moves; artificially imposed trends will resolve into sudden reversals.

Such "**arrival at peace**" refers to a return to the natural state rather than peaceful existence. The market left to its own device, like Nature, is not idyllic. It however operates accordingly to pristine uncorrupted laws of human reactions, thus it becomes a more favorable environment for the skillful trader.

40.
The Principle of Reversion

Reversion is the action of Tao.
Gentleness is the function of Tao.
The things of this world come from Being,
And Being (comes) from Non-being.

We've discussed the Principle of Reversion in earlier chapters as the natural alternating cycles of growth and decay in all phenomena. Together with the Principle of Oneness, the Principle of Reversion constitutes the key to understanding Nature's laws and patterns – namely, the unity and interaction of opposites. Taoism's famous Yin/Yang symbol represents this concept,

Reversion is the action of Tao.

The logic of all phenomena being composed of opposite forces, at first glance, seems contradictory yet becomes evident when tested in practice. We know what light is because we know what dark is. If we had no concept of either one, how could we understand the other? Think about it, if you were completely blind from birth, only knowing darkness, how could you understand light? Because of the blindness you could not contrast or compare anything to the darkness you've always known. Therefore, you could not truly understand the darkness either. To truly understand natural phenomena, you must appreciate how opposites are actually part of the same thing.

Rotation is essential for proper operation. A complete cycle between light and darkness creates the 24-hour day. Crops need the alternation of day time and the circle of seasons. We require sleep to replenish the energy for our awakened state. Any phenomenon depends on its reverse to function properly.

Acknowledgment and acceptance of this principle is part of a realistic view of life as constant change. Good times must be calmly accepted, while some bad times should be anticipated. By anticipating the inevitable rotation, we can prepare. Preparation is imperative to adaptability.

Accepting duality as the basis of all things, Taoists do not brand the developments as "good" or "evil" in an ethical sense – they simply acknowledge the necessity of both for the world to function.

Gentleness is the function of Tao.

"Gentleness" here is more accurately interpreted as adaptation, adjusting to surrounding forces and going with their flow.

The things of this world come from Being,
And Being (comes) from Non-being.

Everything in the world, from the largest to the smallest of manifestations, from the Universe to the individual is the subject to the Principle of Reversion. Any phenomenon is composed of a dualistic relationship of gyrating opposite forces. The states of being and non-being are not separate; they are two sides of the same phenomenon which arises, grows, deteriorates and dies in its eternal cycle.

Reversion is the action of Tao.

Principles described in this poem were discussed extensively in previous chapters, particularly ***2. The Rise of Relative Opposites*** and ***16. Knowing the Eternal Law.*** Let's list the practical applications of these principles. Having discussed them in details earlier, we want to review them briefly, to refresh them in memory and to put it all together.

The most obvious application is of course the **switch between bull and bear phases** of the market. There is no practical way for the market to remain one-directional. Upward movement prepares the ground for the future decline as every current buyer becomes a potential seller. Both directions serve their purposes, thus none of them is good or bad.

Understanding that the process of market movement consists of two sides on any time frame, arms a Taoist Trader with the patience to wait for the right entry. As the market moves farther, an impatient trader will try to enter as soon as possible in fear of missing the opportunity. The astute trader knows that a pullback will come and present him with a much safer and more profitable opportunity. He will wait for the market to come to him, and allow him an entry on his terms – if he stays patient and waits for the natural laws to do their job.

Knowing that no trend will stay there forever, a wise trader will be on the lookout for the signs of a trend reversal, to exit his position and not to overstay his welcome. While a market participant prone to listening to agenda-backed or misguided opinions may believe that one-directional movement is going to continue for much longer (remember our oil run-up example from earlier chapters), a Taoist Trader will remain suspicious of such propaganda. The price action diverging from the commonly accepted view will alert him that the trend is about to change.

A Taoist Trader will understand another instance of this principle applied to trading: **losing trades as an unavoidable part of the trading** process. Winning streaks will yield to losses as sure as day will yield to night. It is important to understand this inevitability, be prepared for it, stay calm and manage risk to make sure that losses remain as small as possible. It is impractical and even harmful to try and avoid losses altogether. Attempts to do so will lead to a refusal to take a loss, thus laying the ground work for the loss to grow beyond reasonable limits. Alternatively, attempt to improve the trading system to "loss-proof" it will lead to endless tweaking with a non-achievable purpose in mind.

It is also important to remember that **each side of the cycle relies on the opposite side for its very existence**. An uptrend-in-waiting need today's sellers so they become tomorrow's buyers that will give a birth to an uptrend. A downtrend-to-be needs today's buyers so they become tomorrow's sellers and launch a downtrend. Trend continuation needs a pullback to attract new players by offering more favorable prices; these new buyers will fuel a new thrust. A winning strategy needs losses to alert a trader that conditions change and it's time to adjust to the new reality – thanks to those losses a strategy remains a winning one through adaptation.

Gentleness is the function of Tao.

Adaptation to the surroundings and going with the natural flow is the crucial trait for a trader. The current of the market will alwaysbe stronger than you. No successful trader ever made a career by remaining stubborn and rigid. Being flexible, being capable of change is an absolute necessity for a trader's survival. We have spoken before of market information being impossible to know in full. That means that there is always a possibility for a surprise turn of events, for an unforeseen twist and simply for being wrong. Staying humble, knowing that our knowledge is inherently limited, remembering that the market is always right, a Taoist Trader remains true to the Taoist principles and free to follow them.

The things of this world come from Being,
And Being (comes) from Non-being.

Deep understanding of natural cycles keeps a wise trader equally capable of taking any side of the trade. To him, there is no difference between long (perceived by many as good) or short (propagandized as evil) – both sides have an equal right to exist, constitute necessary parts of the natural cycle and have no emotional or ethical value attached to them. An upward direction comes from the low price and low volume, from market participants' indifference – all that can be seen as non-existence of the stock or sector in question on traders' radar, total absence of interest. Uptrend ends in euphoria – state where everyone wants to buy the trading vehicle at any price, the summit of interest; such a state can well be characterized as non-existence of any negativity. Knowing that ***Being comes from Non-being***, a Taoist Trader looks for such extremes to spot the moment of reversal – uptrend yielding to downtrend and vice versa. The same cycle occurs with any trading vehicle – currency, commodity, stock or sector: total lack of attention slowly turns into passing interest transforming to full awareness to passion, and then going through the reversal process of losing luster – diminishing excitement turning into mere acknowledgement and going into oblivion. Of course, the whole cycle repeats itself at some point in the future.

Once again, notice how each side depends on the opposite – it is absence of interest that makes it easy for the first buyers to start accumulating their position since there is little to no competition. In the same fashion, it is a lack of negativity that makes it easy for sellers to distribute their shares.

There are important practical conclusions to be made from this observation. Initial buying will be done by experienced traders very carefully, to keep away unwanted attention and get a chance to accumulate as big a position as possible before attracting other buyers. Thus, to spot the start of an uptrend in an inactive issue, a trader must be on the lookout for a careful quiet accumulation, with slowly increasing volume and price rising steadily and moderately. Another important conclusion is that to liquidate a large position easily, one needs to do that while buying enthusiasm is at its highest – in trader-speak this principle is known as "sell when you can, not when you have to."

44.
Be Content

Fame or one's own self, which does one love more?
One's own self or material goods, which has more worth?
Loss (of self) or possession (of goods), which is the greater evil?
Therefore: he who loves most spends most,
He who hoards much loses much.
The contented man meets no disgrace;
Who knows when to stop runs into no danger–
He can long endure.

Personal contentment is the primary goal of Taoism. Unlike many theologies offering rewards in the afterlife, Taoism's approach calls for contentment achieved in daily life. A healthy mental state is a necessary condition for one's good physical health, and increased contentment helps maintain a good mental state.

Contentment requires satisfaction with what one has. Stress and mental anguish arises from endlessly striving for more material possessions and other trappings of success.

Fame or one's own self, which does one love more?
One's own self or material goods, which has more worth?

This stanza cautions that striving for "fame" pressures us to "keep up with the Joneses." Fame among peers requires displaying similar material possessions, skills or social status. Such pressure breeds discontentment. While encouraging the attainment of wealth or social position, peer and societal pressure do not suggest contentment as a goal or measurement of success. Taoists neutralize this pressure by recognizing that all possessions are "loaned" to us and have no permanency. Thus, sacrificing daily contentment for possessions is a chase for borrowed items.

Loss (of self) or possession (of goods), which is the greater evil?

The "loss of self" occurs by sacrificing the present moment for the future. Because reality only exists in the Now, not being fully committed to the present you rob yourself of precious life and "self." Focus on the future trains the individual to forfeit the current moment for some hypothetical promise. The past is filled with moments of discontent, and the present is filled with expectations of the future. The Now ceases to exist. This conduct fractures concentration on the events at hand.

Therefore: he who loves most spends most.
He who hoards much loses much.

A truly content individual relishes life and earns money to fully enjoy each moment. A discontent person hoards his assets for future possibilities. His discontent comes from the loss – loss of forfeited present moments. Unlike money which can be lost and earned again, time cannot be recovered – once lost, it's gone forever.

The contented man meets no disgrace;
Who knows when to stop runs into no danger -
He can long endure.

As a Taoist, if you are content, public disapproval ("disgrace") for limiting desires won't sway you. By ignoring the pressure of society and operating within your limits, you don't overstretch yourself to attain unneeded things and thus avoid danger.

This chapter will take us beyond trading, into something most trading psychology books never discuss. Just as personal contentment is the primary goal of Taoism, trading should naturally lead to personal contentment. Too many traders allow trading to turn into more than their profession or part-time money-making endeavor. It takes up a disproportional part of their lives, becoming an emotional and intellectual burden. Such imbalance is unhealthy and unproductive; it takes an individual farther from his goal of reaching contentment instead of helping him to achieve it.

Unlike true passion, which can have quite a positive influence on one's life even when it consumes a large part of his time, aforementioned imbalance brings discontent and bitterness. You can easily tell the difference by observing the tone of late-night internet discussions by the individual in question: most of them are angry and irritated, assigning blame for his failed trades. Emotionally balanced content trader will normally be busy with other aspects of his life rather than express his anger to strangers online.

It is important for a trader to remember the place of trading in his life. Living happily in the Now is act of an accomplished Taoist Trader. Replacing today's happiness with tomorrow's goals is foolish. Trading is but a part of the wholesome life – there is family, friends, hobbies, travel and whatever else one enjoys. Make trading your tool for achieving your goals, instead of allowing it to become a substitute for those goals and overtake your life.

For trading to be a natural part of your life, it should not be an alienating experience. Although there will be, especially at the first stages, disappointing and aggravating parts to it, it is important to maintain a level attitude and make a conscious deliberate effort to integrate it into your life in an organic fashion. There are a few things a Taoist Trader can do to achieve this.

First is forming the right expectations. Recalling that desires and expectations are at the core of suffering, one must realize that trading is not and can not be easy. It is a profession, as large and complicated as any other, and in some ways more than many others. It is also a business where one is fully responsible for the performance. Looking in the monitor every day is in some ways like looking in the mirror. It is also a process of self-learning and self-change. It would be completely unrealistic to expect to become proficient at it overnight or within mere months. Keeping expectations reasonable helps one remain level-headed and avoid disappointments. Many aspects taught by Taoism, such as humility and the impossibility to comprehend the whole system around us, help us understand and remember our role and place in the market, thus keeping our expectations within rational limits.

Second is learning the right mindset. We have discussed calmness earlier in Chapter 37. ***World Peace***. It is also imperative to maintain a positive mental attitude, create room for humor in your daily trading routine and make sure you view everything that happens with a good degree of detachment. Self-deprecating jokes go a long way in keeping you grounded and allowing you to maintain the right perspective.

Third is making sure you don't let trading-related activities overtake your life. Make sure you find time for everything you enjoy. Entertain your friends, spend time with your family, enjoy your favorite hobbies – and be sure to be totally in the moment, enjoying all these activities fully and being engaged. Remember that trading is a sedentary activity – make sure to get enough physical activity as well.

Trading can and should be an enjoyable endeavor. One rarely can become good at something he doesn't enjoy. Think of what it is in trading that you like – not just making money but some part of the process that brings you satisfaction. Is it an act of successful self-control? Is it masterful reading of the market mood? Is it the very process of the intellectual contest, engaging in The Game? Make a deliberate effort to remember the enjoyable part, focus on it, and keep yourself in a state of taking pleasure in it. This act by itself will help keep stress levels down and increase your productivity.

Fame or one's own self, which does one love more?
One's own self or material goods, which has more worth?

In light of the above paragraphs, this stanza's meaning becomes transparent. To remain content, a Taoist Trader does not pursue a goal of making as much money as someone else does or making predictions to impress his peers. Instead, he sets his goals based on his actual needs and limitations. Banning vanity and pride from his psyche, he remains grounded in reality. This approach allows him to perform at the optimal level and stay content and relaxed, avoiding meaningless competition with Joneses.

Loss (of self) or possession (of goods), which is the greater evil?

That content life will occur NOW, not in some undefined future. A Taoist Trader cherishes every moment, not letting his hopes for the better future rob him of today's happiness. Living full and balanced life today and every day is true objective.

Focusing on the present during trading process is also a necessary condition for profitable trading. Too much focus on attempts to foresee market actions with little regard for what happens at the moment can be devastating for one's trading account. In trading, it's not enough to be right about market direction – it's crucial to be right at the right moment. You can see traders complaining about predicting certain market action correctly but still losing money by "being too early" – this is a prime example of the market doling out punishment for the concentration on some undetermined future with no regard for timing.

Therefore: he who loves most spends most.
He who hoards much loses much.

A truly content trader takes pleasure in his today and earns money to fully enjoy each moment. A discontent person hoards his assets for future possibilities. His disgruntlement comes from the loss of forfeited present moments. Money which can be lost and earned again; lost time cannot be recovered. Avoid substituting tools for a goal – trading is but a tool for reaching your goals, not the goal in itself.

The contented man meets no disgrace;
Who knows when to stop runs into no danger -
He can long endure.

As a Taoist Trader, if you are content, you won't be swayed by public disapproval ("**disgrace**") for keeping your expectations grounded. The pressure of peers in trading often is expressed in comparing profits, position size and derisive remarks aimed at those who don't trade "big" and keeps his objectives modest. A wise trader will recognize such pressure for what it is – vanity and arrogance, empty competition aimed to satisfy one's pride. Understanding the true motives behind such behavior and the harm it can do to one's mindset, he will dismiss it and remain true to his inner purposes.

54.
The Individual and the State

Who is firmly established is not easily shaken.
Who has a firm grasp does not easily let go.
From generation to generation his ancestral sacrifices
Shall be continued without fail.
Cultivated in the individual, character will become genuine;
Cultivated in the family, character will become abundant;
Cultivated in the village, character will multiply;
Cultivated in the state, character will prosper;
Cultivated in the world, character will become universal.
Therefore :
According to (the character of) the individual, judge the individual;
According to (the character of) the family, judge the family;
According to (the character of) the village, judge the village;
According to (the character of) the state, judge the state;
According to (the character of) the world, judge the world;
How do I know the world is so.
By this.

Taoism is distinctive as a philosophy that speaks of the injurious effects of the social structure on an individual. A society's propaganda machine promotes values that serve its interests. ***The Individual and the State*** *focuses on how one's personality is shaped by society's ladder, beginning with the individual himself and continuing with the family, the community, the state, and the world, at large. In Lao Tzu's view, in the conduct of our lives, we are the ruler of our own realm.*

Who is firmly established is not shaken.
Who has a firm grasp does not easily let go.

These first few lines refer to the Taoist being a free thinker, taking nothing on faith and checking everything by practical application. The average man, on the opposite, follows society's instructions and makes decisions based on common beliefs adopted by the majority. Lack of critical thinking makes members of the crowd indistinguishable. Their comfort is found in convention to which they commit with absolute confidence that "is not shaken" nor "easily let go."

From generation to generation his ancestral sacrifices
Shall be continued without fail.

One of the elements of societal indoctrination is traditional worship towards ancestors, whose achievements and qualities are glorified routinely. There is a grave belief in traditional values transferred from generation to generation, regardless of their practical applicability to modern circumstances.

Cultivated in the individual, character will become genuine;

Character consists of the individual's moral and ethical traits. There is a profound difference between building one's character using the values observed in nature, versus those taught by the society. A Taoist, not accepting beliefs and notions automatically, constantly challenges himself with the question, "Why?" Any decision is being weighed by the all-encompassing criteria: Is this right for me as an individual? A Taoist does things because they make sense, not because everyone else does them. If we concentrate on developing ourselves as individuals, our moral and ethical values will be genuine, not imposed from outside. Our decisions and actions will then be based on reality and not on someone else's interests.

Cultivated in the family, character will become abundant;

This line speaks of the principle of the Taoist cocoon – circle of people sharing the same beliefs and values, not necessarily those with whom we share genetic lineage.

Cultivated in the village, character will multiply;
Cultivated in the state, character will prosper;
Cultivated in the world, character will become universal.

In the hierarchy outlined by Lao Tzu, individual must find his place and role in the community ("village"), the state and the world that promote their priorities. In order to function properly and prosper, we need to develop ourselves as individuals, while working within societal structures and limitations. This requires the Taoist to cultivate his "Third Eye" – a skill of looking through the eyes of others. Understanding how you are seen helps the individual understand their fit in the society around them so they can respond appropriately to a given situation.

As the state and the world are much bigger than us as individuals, we need to use disguise so as to not draw unnecessary attention. One of the basic doctrines of Taoism is to never contend with the social structures, keeping in line with one of Taoism's cardinal tenets, non-interference.

Therefore :
According to (the character of) the individual, judge the individual;
According to (the character of) the family, judge the family;

According to (the character of) the village, judge the village;
According to (the character of) the state, judge the state;
According to (the character of) the world, judge the world;

These lines all deal with the same central theme – evaluate the character of an individual, family, village, state and the world, by testing them to make sure that proposed values or ideas are genuine and not manipulative propaganda. A Taoist will validate everything through practical application, not relying on pure faith .

How do I know the world is so.
By this.

The end of this stanza again carries a message about being "results oriented." "By this" means that any theoretical discussion must lead to some practical result. The principle is useful if it produces positive result. Clever promoters can make any idea sound plausible; practical application must be the only real validation.

TAOISM'S concepts remind us that the market, while rich in opportunities, is not an environment structured for an individual's benefit. While a trader can make a living or even a fortune unimpeded, it can be done only by independent thinking instead of following the common views. As market information flows and propaganda promotes interests of various participants and organizations, by no means is it aimed at making any listener rich. Being a "ruler of our own realm" requires critical, even skeptical, thinking that puts us in charge of our own actions.

Who is firmly established is not shaken.
Who has a firm grasp does not easily let go.

A Taoist trader, being a free thinker, takes nothing on pure faith and checks everything by practical application. The average member of the trading crowd follows common beliefs and notions and makes decisions based on the opinions expressed by various gurus, commentators and media personalities. It is those opinions adopted by the majority, seemingly so obvious and non-arguable, lead to the self-damaging actions repeated by the blind followers over and over again. No matter how many times in the past such actions proved to be harmful for the financial health of the market participants, crowds continue following the conventional path of self-destruction. Be it the Tulip Mania or the South Sea bubble of past centuries, or the tech boom or housing bubble of modern times, a crowd's behavior stays the same. It is this same behaviorthat form chart patterns that work today as they did decades ago It is a crowd's emotional action that causes capitulation sell-offs – panicky "get me out at any price" while fear is being propagated by each and every commentator. It is a crowd's emotional action that causes euphoria spikes – elated "just want to be on board no matter the price" while unbridled optimism is being promoted by those same commentators. Time and again following such propaganda leaves the crowds buying the top and selling the bottom. Stunning rallies come after the panic rids the investors of their shares; dramatic market drops appear after the masses throw caution to the wind and buy everything in sight. Lack of critical thinking makes members of the crowd indistinguishable and leads them to repetitive self-destructive behavior. They are "***firmly established***" and "***not shaken***" in their beliefs; it is that firm confidence of which a Taoist trader is so cautious. Understanding how crowds that can't "easily let go" act provides astute traders with ample opportunity in the markets. Rigid confidence in dogmas impedes flexibility of mind; healthy skepticism allows for acceptance of error even in commonly acknowledged "facts."

From generation to generation his ancestral sacrifices
Shall be continued without fail.

Reference to certain market-related "wisdom" as being old and proven should not stop a Taoist Trader from questioning it. After all, claims like "in the long run the market always goes up" or "don't try to time the market," which we have shown to be false in earlier chapters, have been propagated long enough to be considered quite old. That doesn't make them any closer to the truth though.

The only true criteria for any method are practical application and real life performance. Deep understanding of the principles on which the market is based allows a trader to see whether the suggested approach is based on those principles or constitutes an artificial attempt to impose someone's will on the market. Such an attempt will unavoidably fail as real laws of the market inevitably take over.

Cultivated in the individual, character will become genuine;

To be sound and effective a trader's approach and mindset must be built on true market laws and patterns, instead of the dogmas propagated by entities with their own agenda. A Taoist Trader constantly verifies opinions and notions to select those that make sense, that benefit his trading performance. Being offered, for instance, to "hang tight and not to sell at loss because market is sure to reverse soon" he will dismiss such advice knowing that allowing his loss to grow uncontrollably can terminate his trading career. Seeing that such advice is given by the author of a trading idea that now shows a loss, he will recognize the agenda behind the advice: the desire to prove to the audience the idea was right, the refusal to admit an error, and their injured ego needing validation. A wise trader will be able to predict what the guru is going to do next if the market continues proving him wrong: he will blame the manipulators that ruined his perfectly good trading idea. Whatever it does for a guru in question, it's certainly harmful for a trader, thus he will not follow the guru's recommendation.

A Taoist Trader never does things because everyone else does them. His beliefs and notions must be genuine and based on observable reality. Any opinions followed by the masses will be inherently suspicious to him.

Cultivated in the family, character will become abundant;

Just as the Taoist's cocoon – circle of those sharing the same beliefs and values – includes a fairly limited number of people, a Taoist Trader will usually find that there is a narrow circle of those who approach the market similarly. Such people will be guided by healthy self-interest and will value the co-operation with a few like-minded.

Cultivated in the village, character will multiply;
Cultivated in the state, character will prosper;
Cultivated in the world, character will become universal.

The idea of the "Third Eye" – a skill of looking through the eyes of others, or from the outside – finds an application in trading. We touched on this earlier in Chapter 14 ***Prehistoric Origin***s. This skill allows a trader to view the events in the market through the eyes on other participants, thus foreseeing their probable reactions. He uses his own emotions as a mirror to the emotions of the trading masses – only being a disciplined practitioner of Taoism in the market, he is capable of separating his actions from his emotions.

How do I know the world is so.
By this.

This stanza once again emphasizes the necessity of practical verification for any trading method suggested or promoted by other participants. Many trading strategies are promoted in a very clever way, equipped with falsified "proof" of performance constructed in a believable manner. They promise easy riches with minimum to no work required; they are outfitted with testimonials and refer to industry authorities that recommend them. A Taoist Trader will recognize that no method can bring a reward to anyone who buys the offered system and puts it to use with no work on their own. Practical verification is the only real way to check the system performance, not blind faith for a vendor's hype.

63. Difficult and Easy

Accomplish do-nothing.
Attend to no-affairs.
Taste the flavorless.
Whether it is big or small, many or few,
Requite hatred with virtue.
Deal with the difficult while yet it is easy;
Deal with the big while yet it is small.
The difficult (problems) of the world
Must be dealt with while they are yet easy;
The great (problems) of the world
Must be dealt with while they are yet small.
Therefore the Sage by never dealing with great (problems)
Accomplishes greatness.
He who lightly makes a promise
Will find it often hard to keep his faith.
He who makes light of many things
Will encounter many difficulties.
Hence even the Sage regards things as difficult,
And for that reason never meets with difficulties

The seriousness and size of the problems we encounter often increase when the problems are left unaddressed so they develop and grow. The sooner you see a problem coming, the easier it will be to fix it. Regular maintenance prevents major repairs; addressing minor health problem prevents major disease, and taking care of trivial misunderstandings prevents relationship damage. Symptoms, no matter how small, should not be taken lightly.

Accomplish do-nothing.
Attend to no-affairs.
Taste the flavorless.

This refers to the Principle of Wu Wei, which we've discussed in prior chapters. Taoists try to avoid creating problems by not interfering with things without necessity. Following our path and allowing others to fulfill their original natures, we allow things to develop their natural way.

Whether it is big or small, many or few,
Requite hatred with virtue.

In this stanza, Lao Tzu instructs the individual to approach each problem, no matter how small, with the same vigor and attention. Practicing small issue detection is good training to detect things that could grow large. Big issues are called to our attention naturally, but we often forget big problems stem from the small. Applying the same process on simple issues, we learn how to handle the complicated. Paying attention to insignificant troubles, we are able to spot potentially large ones early.

Such an approach also pays tribute to our personal built-in limitations. Extreme diligence reflects an understanding that we need to spot changes before they exceed our limited abilities to deal with them.

Lao Tzu also warns us not to let emotions, "hatred," dictate our actions. Decisions made under the influence of strong passions often lead to bigger problems. Emotions also cloud our sensitivity to what's happening. Solutions suggested with a calm demeanor are likely to be accepted by other participants more willingly.

Deal with the difficult while yet it is easy;
Deal with the big while yet it is small.

Reiterating the poem's theme, big problems almost always start as smaller ones. Small problems are always easier to solve then big problems. The main question becomes, how to recognize the problem early. The answer lies in recognizing the repeated patterns through the application of Taoist principles, which leads to developing sensitivity to unfolding events. Understanding how things are likely to develop allows one to catch the problems "while yet it is easy." This approach does not call for paranoia but rather a detached observation of early symptoms. Of course, all cases do not require reaction and in many instances the best decision is to let things develop along their natural course. It is however important to recognize problems and prepare for action. Then, if it becomes necessary, when the right moment comes, we are ready and have designed course of action.

The difficult (problems) of the world
Must be dealt with while they are yet easy;
The great (problems) of the world
Must be dealt with while they are yet small.
Therefore the Sage by never dealing with great (problems)
Accomplishes greatness.

Never having to address great problems is possible for The Sage because he identifies and resolves them before they become big.

He who lightly makes a promise
Will find it often hard to keep his faith.
He who makes light of many things

Will encounter many difficulties.
Hence even the Sage regards things as difficult,
And for that reason never meets with difficulties.

Those who make promises without understanding the gravity of the situation may find it difficult to keep their commitments. Lack of sensitivity to the scale of the problem and to the probable course of its development causes misjudgment of both the problem, and one's limitations in dealing with it. Taking problem lightly, not recognizing its potential to grow into much bigger troubles leads to ***"encountering many difficulties."*** *Regarding things as potentially difficult, even when they are simple, and taking them seriously helps prevent that so one* ***"never meet with difficulties."***

IN trading, it is very important to stay sensitive to the upcoming changes and deal with small problems not letting them turn into large ones. Let's cite examples of this approach and analyze how it benefits a Taoist Trader.

The most glaring application of this principle is limiting one's losses. Dealing with a loss **while yet it is small** guarantees that it never becomes an issue jeopardizing your whole trading account. A Taoist Trader combines two principles in dealing with a trade that develops adversely.

First is Wu Wei – non-interference. It's applied while the price moves against his position but hasn't hit a stop level yet. Such a move is just a natural volatility and does not call for action, thus our trader "**accomplishes do-nothing** and **attends to no-affairs.**" Hectic reaction on any tick would qualify as intrusion without necessity and create a problem by itself, causing liquidation of a position for no good reason, reinitiating a new position and overtrading.

Second is being prepared to cut the loss if and when a trade failure becomes obvious in terms of one's trading system. Stop placement is predetermined; signs of trade failure are strictly defined. When a moment to acts comes, action is taken decisively and the problem is dealt with **while yet it is easy.**

To complete the analysis, let's compare this approach with behavior of a trader who ignores this principle and see where it takes him. As his predetermined stop level is hit, the loss is small in size, thus does not feel alarming. If a stop is placed correctly with regards to market's volatility, trading pattern, position size and trading account size, that's exactly what is supposed to happen – the loss should not be disturbingly large, nor should it cause emotional pain. This however tempts a trader to try and wait things out, and rationalize his "small yet" loss in the hope his position recovers. As the loss grows (as it well should in most cases since the trading pattern is broken), a trader starts feeling pain. Now he is hoping for the price to return to his original stop level, to take a lesser loss than he faces at the moment. Needless to say, emotions run high at this point and start influencing all his decisions. There is no saying what he does next; one thing is obvious though – whatever it is it's not likely to be rational. At some point a trader decides that the loss is too big now to take, as his trading account would be damaged too deeply. In most cases he ends up taking the loss nonetheless, when it grows larger yet and pains exceeds his threshold of tolerance. To add insult to injury, this moment all too often coincides with a market reversal. The damage is hard to overestimate:

- a trading account has taken a hard hit;
- many profitable opportunities came and went unnoticed and unexploited while he was nurturing his loss;
- confidence in his trading abilities is damaged badly;
- emotional disturbance ruined his balance, causing anger, extreme aggravation and a spectrum of negative sentiments.

All this frustration and financial distress started with the refusal to deal with a small loss at the very beginning.

Another application of the principle is in trend reversals. For a trend following trader who took his position, counting on a movement continuing, it becomes important to watch for the signs of trend reversal. Just as in the previous example, a Taoist Trader balances two principles. Again, first is Wu Wei – a trader does not react on any downtick (in his time frame of course – for a long term trader downtick means a red day, for a day trader it can be a red bar on one minute chart). By **accomplishing do-nothing** he avoids overtrading and cutting his profits too early. He however stays on the lookout for signs of a trend turnaround, be it a chart pattern of technical indicators signaling danger. Preparing for action and staying sensitive to the signs of nascent problems allows him to secure his profits.

Once again, let's look at the action of a trader who ignores such signs. Convinced that favorable price action will continue, he ignores the first signs of a problem. To help visualize such a situation, let's recall a very recent example – peak of the oil prices in the summer of 2008 at $147.27. All kinds of prognoses for the trend to continue were made everywhere with price targets at $200, $300 etc. Price however started declining. By itself, it wouldn't be a reason to exit the trade – no trend goes in a straight line without pullbacks. However, a series of lower highs and lower lows made against the backdrop of calls for a further run-up was a strong warning sign. This is where that extremely damaging emotional cycle started developing for those who ignored early signs of troubles. While the retreat from the high was relatively small (about $22 over first two weeks), it was easy to ignore. In a month, it dropped to $112 – $35 decline. Such cut in profits was harder to accept, and many traders started convincing themselves that they had to sit it out, rationalizing their decision by all kinds of fundamental explanations for the inevitable and imminent price rise. In about two months, the price broke below $100. Vicious destruction of hopes and trading accounts continued for a few months more, taking the price under $40 (!) before a rebound finally started. Curiously enough (although not at all unpredictable), as the price declined that much, negative predictions became overwhelming, calling for even lower prices and causing desperate holders to bail out – close to eventual bottom, of course.

The third application of the "**dealing with easy before it becomes difficult**" principle can be seen in the idea of monitoring one's performance to spot the moment when the market changes significantly enough to signal when some tweaks to your trading system are warranted. It may not mean a complete makeover of course – just switch to a different chart pattern, change of expectations etc. Nothing stays the same forever, and even the most successful trading approach requires certain adjustments as the market moves through the cycles of activity, trends, volume and volatility. As with earlier examples, a Taoist Trader will spot the change early and prepare the necessary changes, to spring into action when necessary. Using the template we applied in the first two examples, you can reproduce the development of events for both traders – one who stays alert and one who dismisses the early warning signs.

To recognize the small changes early and estimate their potential correctly, a trader has to stay emotionally detached (**Requite hatred with virtue**). Being too committed to an existing position or a trading idea, developing emotional involvement leaves us with subjective outlook and leads to rationalization – much like oil traders convinced themselves oil had nowhere to go but up.

Therefore the Sage by never dealing with great (problems)
Accomplishes greatness.

This part reflects itself in a phenomenon you can often observe in great traders. They seem to never, or rarely, encounter difficulties. For a side observer it looks like they are somehow protected from the problems most traders encounter regularly. It is of course an illusion – a Taoist Trader is subject to all the same problems the market presents. However, by staying alert, recognizing the potential problems and dealing with them **while they are yet small** a wise trader escapes unscathed, avoiding the brunt of accumulating difficulties.

67.
The Three Treasures

All the world says: my teaching (Tao) greatly resembles folly.
Because it is great; therefore it resembles folly.
If it did not resemble folly,
It would have long ago become petty indeed!
I have Three Treasures;
Guard them and keep them safe:
the first is Love.
The second is, Never too much.
The third is, Never be the first in the world.
Through Love, one has no fear;
Through not doing too much, one has amplitude
(of reserve power);
Through not presuming to be the first in the world,
One can develop one's talent and let it mature.
If one forsakes love and fearlessness,
forsakes restraint and reserve power,
forsakes following behind and rushes in front,
He is doomed!
For love is victorious in attack,
And invulnerable in defense.
Heaven arms with love
Those it would not see destroyed.

*The **Three Treasures** present several concise recommendations to apply in daily life. Their implications are important in Taoist thinking and combine a broad philosophical outlook with every day pragmatism.*

All the world says: my teaching (Tao) greatly resembles folly.
Because it is great; therefore it resembles folly.

This stanza emphasizes the contrary nature of Taoist principles. Taking the opposite stance to prevailing social values, A Taoist is seen as eccentric by those who uphold conventional views.

If it did not resemble folly,
It would have long ago become petty indeed!

If the powerful truth of Taoism had been obvious, it would have been subjugated by the establishment and distorted to fit their objectives. Social structures, when encountering ideas threatening the status quo, will often redefine them to serve their needs and implement them in a form that advances their purposes.

I have Three Treasures;
Guard them and keep them safe:
The first is Love.

As we mentioned in the Preface, interpretation of Lao Tzu's writings are often far from obvious. Practical application will identify mistaken understandings. This stanza is a perfect example of erroneous interpretation: the western version of "love" makes no sense when one considers the poem's final stanza:

For love is victorious in attack,
And invulnerable in defense.
Heaven arms with love
Those it would not see destroyed.

However poetic it may sound, a philosophy as pragmatic as Taoism must have had some other meaning for this term. One must understand that there is no term in most Asian languages for the western/Christian concept of love. The word is merely the closest approximation translators can find for the Chinese characters. Lao Tzu's definition of "love" includes three concepts.

First is acceptance. That which we love, we unconditionally accept for what it is – be it a friend, relative or job. A professional must accept his vocation as interesting and exciting to achieve excellence. Partial commitment won't lead to significant achievements. A surgeon disliking his profession and performing surgeries because it's a good source of income is not a professional to whom you would want to trust your health. The concept of acceptance also applies to the battleground. Embracing a situation as a dangerous clash, where no wishing or pleading will resolve the conflict, is necessary to deal with it effectively.

The second aspect of Lao Tzu's concept of "love" is simplicity. As a situation is accepted, choices become unambiguous. In a conflict, you're either the predator or the prey; your choices are to fight, flee or surrender. The ability to analyze situations and list one's options in a simple fashion is a powerful technique helping navigate every day life. It is one of the crucial tools for removing confusion and cutting down stress.

The third concept contained in Lao Tzu's notion of "love" is caring action. After you accept something and outline your options, the next step is practical implementation.

To sum it up, Lao Tzu's First Treasure prescribes "love" in the battlefield of life, instructing us to accept the reality of situations, simplify our options, and then act with passion.

The second is, Never too much.

The second treasure is a warning to avoid excess. Extremes in the physical world generally lead to disaster or deteriorating health. The second treasure, however, is not a suggestion of denial or universal minimization. For just as too much food makes one obese, too little leads to starvation.

Thus, both excess and denial are to be avoided, and the right quantity of anything to do or consume is defined by the necessity or sufficiency. "Never too much" instructs the Taoist to determine and achieve the proper levels in order to function correctly.

The caution also applies in the mental realm. Excessive mental activity results in a disturbed mind that exceedingly worries about life's every possibility. A mind that constantly dwells on life's "ifs" cannot live in the Now; attempts to calculate everything in advance and plan for every turn create endless doubts and fear of the future and paralyze an individual.

The third is, Never be the first in the world.

Lao Tzu's Third Treasure is a caution to shun one of society's urgings – to constantly excel and best those around us. There is an implied message that happiness can only be achieved through being the best, or standing out from the crowd.

Lao Tzu recognized the toxic effects that the perpetual chase of first place has on contentment. Harsh rivalry for status and wealth is one of society's main tools for manipulation, by invoking pride and vanity.

Achieving success and displaying it proudly makes you a target for others in their pursuit for first place. The tallest tree is always the first to be cut down. A Taoist will quietly enjoy material success and lead a content life, without standing out in the crowd.

Through Love, one has no fear;

By using the three-pronged definition of "love" – acceptance, simplicity and passionate action – fear can be effectively managed. These psychological tools equip a Taoist with the strength necessary to handle situations.

Through not doing too much, one has amplitude (of reserve power);

This line advises to use our energy only when necessary, preserving it so you'll have plenty of power when needed.

Through not presuming to be the first in the world,
One can develop one's talent and let it mature.

By not competing for the artificial prizes endorsed by society, the individual can cultivate his natural talents; not getting involved in the exhausting race, he conserves energy and saves time to let his natural inclinations and talents mature without becoming a target of others' jealousy.

If one forsakes love and fearlessness,
forsakes restraint and reserve power,
forsakes following behind and rushes in front,
He is doomed!

This conclusion is a brief summary of the content of the poem.

All the world says: my teaching (Tao) greatly resembles folly.
Because it is great; therefore it resembles folly.

BY now, we are fairly familiar with the idea of contrarian thinking being the cornerstone of a trader's approach. We went extensively over the concept of obvious actions not leading to success in the market (***Chapter 54. The Individual and the State*** and others). Compared to conventional thinking, a trader's thoughts seem odd. He is not looking to buy the market on good news or sell on bad news. Instead, he is looking for the divergence between price action and available information to take position opposite of what the majority does. In other words, when the trading circles embrace en-masse a certain notion about market direction yet the price action does not confirm that notion, a Taoist Trader goes against that widely accepted opinion. He is taking the views expressed by the vocal majority as a signal for contrary action.

If it did not resemble folly,
It would have long ago become petty indeed!

The winning way in the market must be contrarian almost by definition. Obvious action embraced by the majority of market participants becomes the losing action by virtue of being perpetuated by majority. As most of the entities take one side of the trade, they all, in full accordance with Taoist principles, become potential performers for the other side – today's buyers are tomorrow's sellers. Tipping the balance, they give an astute trader a clue to what is coming, so he can take advantage of this understanding by trading against the crowds. Naturally, his views at this moment "**resemble folly**," and if they didn't, they would be erroneous ("**petty**").

I have Three Treasures;
Guard them and keep them safe:
The first is Love.

Now that we are familiar with Lao Tzu's three-pronged definition of "love," let's see how it applies in trading.

The first of three concepts in a Taoist's view is an unconditional acceptance. Just as a professional in any field must accept his craft as captivating and exciting to achieve excellence in his skills, a trader should be fascinated by his field of activity. Many beginning traders perceive the market as an unpleasant environment and trading – as a repulsive activity. Needless to say, it is impossible to achieve success in a vocation perceived as revolting. It's difficult to envision one becoming successful in an environment that instills fear and loathing in him. Just as a surgeon performing an operation as a means to make a living while disliking his profession is not someone you want as your doctor, a trader disapproving of the market can not be expected to be any good at his job. A Taoist Trader will accept the market as his natural environment, one where he feels at home. A trading battlefield is what it is and must be accepted for what it is – fair or not, dangerous yet filled with opportunities, treacherous yet obeying certain patterns that can be observed and exploited. Such acceptance is a necessary condition of effectiveness.

The second aspect of Lao Tzu's concept of "love" is simplicity. A Taoist Trader possesses the ability to simplify the situation and outline his options in a straightforward way. One's trading approach must be simple enough for a trader to see clearly; overcomplicated systems that are difficult to explain, understand, and remember are not very effective. Vagueness in a trading approach is a sure sign of a bad design.

We spoke earlier (***Chapter 24, The Dregs and Tumors of Virtue***) of routines that standardize response to a typical situation. Such routines, among other tasks, are necessary to simplify a trader's choices and make the process of following them automatic. This leads us to the third-concept contained in Lao Tzu's notion of "love" – caring action, or practical implementation.

Let's sum up this concept of "love" as a Taoist Trader's mindset, as it is a very important one. It outlines the whole attitude of a trader, his vision of himself, his surroundings and his place and role in these surroundings.

For love is victorious in attack,
And invulnerable in defense.
Heaven arms with love
Those it would not see destroyed.

A winning trader accepts the market for what it is – a loosely structured highly liquid environment governed by numerous forces interacting in a principally non-computable way, where observable patterns obey the laws of human psychology and defy the false premises of stiff logic. He enjoys the process of deciphering the way Tao manifests itself in the markets; he is enthralled by the elegance and ruthlessness of these manifestations. Armed with understanding of Taoist principles, he cultivates the ability to see his choices clearly and act decisively when the choice is made. His routine actions pre-defined by his trading system outline his options and give him clear instructions. His confidence in his approach and strict risk control, drawn from repeated practice/experience allow him to act without hesitation. This is the way "love" makes him "**victorious in attack and invulnerable in defense**."

The second is, Never too much.

Second Treasure is a warning to avoid excesses. It instructs to avoid both excess and denial, and defines the right levels as necessary for sufficiency.

Trading applications of this principle are multiple. First of all, **Never too much** suggests a trader to be reasonable in his expectations of the size of the market move. An astute trader will be on the lookout for the signs of a trend change and won't let false hopes keep him in a trade longer than necessary (excess), to risk letting his profit evaporate or turn into loss. He will also avoid another extreme (denial) – exiting his position too soon, not letting worthy profits develop.

Second, he will make sure that his position is sized right. Avoiding too big a size (excess), he controls his risk, makes sure he is comfortable, not letting the scale of monetary impact of every tick overwhelm him. On the opposite side lies another extreme to avoid – too small a position that requires an unreasonably big movement to yield any meaningful profit.

Excessive mental activity can cause unneeded commotion and unnecessary worries. A Taoist Trader puts much weight into preliminary preparations. He limits the deliberation during the process of execution to a minimum. Re-thinking pre-canned responses to typical situations is second-guessing, and can lead to hesitation and flawed execution. Equally harmful are attempts to figure out every possible turn of events and prevent every possible danger, leading to so-called "paralysis by analysis." One of the oft-seen symptoms of this erroneous approach is overloading the screens with numerous technical indicators and studies. Overabundance of such tools tends to cloud a trader's perception rather than help it.

A wise trader knows that he can't forecast every possibility (our knowledge of the world is inherently limited), and there is always a risk of running into an unforeseen incident. His task is not to foretell the future but to anticipate the most probable course of development and preserve himself in the event of an adverse scenario. This skill of the "middle ground action" is essential for a trader: taking advantage of the most likely scenario while limiting the risk in the most deadly case, however unlikely it may be. Prepared for these alternatives, thus not needing to figure out each possible turn and twist, a trader can limit his thinking to that which is necessary and sufficient. In typical Taoist fashion, there is a seeming paradox: a trader acting in this way doesn't have to predict the future, yet he is ready to react on any turn of events in the most constructive way possible.

The third is, Never be the first in the world.

We have discussed in previous chapters the futility attempting to be the first and best at everything, thus attracting unwanted attention. Such a course of action dictated by ego is fatal for a trader. A Taoist Trader does not trade to compete – he will never participate in silly contests to prove who is a better trader. Nor will he engage in endless fruitless debates about future market events – he knows very well that no one is able to foresee them, and avoids locking himself up in an expressed opinion that would make his mind rigid. He values the ability to stay flexible and listen to the market; to preserve this ability he would rather sound unsure when discussing possible developments, making his opinion conditional and adding multiple "if" and "unless."

An astute trader will trade within his abilities, which he evaluates as objectively and humbly as possible. He will avoid pushing for excessive fortune, remembering that it is during the pursuit of unachievable goals that one becomes vulnerable.

Through Love, one has no fear;

One of the most paralyzing mental states for a trader is fear. "Scared money can't win," the old traders' saying goes. Fear dictates exactly the wrong course of action. Fear of loss causes a trader to refuse to take a small stop, and leads him to a large one. Fear to lose profit makes him take his position off prematurely, not letting the trade develop. Fear of the unknown trade outcome can lead to a refusal to engage – the condition known as "gun-shy." Finally, fear of the market in general creates stress that weighs heavily on a trader's mental state and negatively influences his performance and entire life.

By using the aforementioned three-pronged definition of "love" – acceptance, simplicity and passionate action – fear can be effectively managed. A trader's acceptance of the market for what it is ceases to be a fearsome frightening environment. Simple clear actions outlined in an unambiguous way give him the decisiveness to act. Prepared, automated, routine responses to recognizable situations enable him to act without hesitation. Thus, "**Through Love, one has no fear**."

Through not doing too much, one has amplitude (of reserve power);

One of the crucial skills for a trader is to stay inactive when there are no opportunities present. We spoke plenty about the ability to act decisively when the time comes. Such times are defined as recognizable situations – certain chart setups, certain events etc. – in which a trader knows the odds stack up in his favor. However, when no such situation presents itself, it's another standard situation in a trader's arsenal for which he must have a trained response – do nothing. It can be a daunting task, to sit and wait for the right opportunity while the market moves up and down, money is made and lost and it feels like time is wasted. Impatience can easily take over, causing a trader to abandon his routine and jump in the middle of the action. A Taoist Trader knows to pick his battles and wait for the one he can manage.

69.
Camouflage

There is the maxim of military strategists;
I dare not be the first to invade, but rather be the invaded.
Dare not press forward an inch, but rather retreat a foot.
That is, to march without formations,
To roll not up the sleeves,
to charge not in frontal attacks,
To arm without weapons.
There is no greater catastrophe than to underestimate the enemy.
To underestimate the enemy might entail the loss of my treasures.
Therefore when two equally matched armies meet,
It is the man of sorrow who wins.

Camouflage in earlier chapters was mentioned in the context of fitting into society without creating unnecessary friction. This poem discusses another angle: how camouflage is used in a conflict. While the Taoist principle of non-interference teaches us to avoid unnecessary confrontations, conflict sometimes becomes unavoidable. Our inability to predict the future means that there will be unexpected developments during the conflict.

Risk is much more manageable if we let potential adversaries expose their intentions. This presents us with better opportunity to study the challenge and work out a suitable response. Humility in assuming that the enemy is stronger than oneself is a better ally than pride leading to not underestimating the opponent.

There is the maxim of military strategists;
I dare not be the first to invade, but rather be the invaded.

Letting an adversary come to our terrain and engage on our terms is often a better tactic, allowing one to prepare on familiar ground. Defense also requires less force, allowing one to save the resources for a counter-attack while an enemy has the majority of his war assets committed to resource-demanding offense.

Dare not press forward an inch, but rather retreat a foot.

Temporary retreat to consolidate our position draws an aggressor to his disadvantage, opening an opportunity for us. It's a much smarter tactic than aggressive posturing – empty bravado doesn't impress worthy adversary.

That is, to march without formations,

*Marching **"without formations"** refers to moving without visible purpose, not exposing our intentions and forces, thus making it more difficult for an opponent to plan.*

To roll not up the sleeves,
to charge not in frontal attacks,

***"Roll not up the sleeves"** instructs us to appear unprepared for conflict, mislead the enemy by appearing to be not aggressive. During actual battle engagement, this stanza suggests to avoid conventionally obvious moves (**"frontal attacks."**)*

Another aspect of camouflage is to keep capabilities hidden instead of displaying them thus revealing information that can be used against us. Publicizing strength or intentions puts us at a disadvantage, bringing unwanted attention and allowing enemy planning. Maintaining a low profile requires both humility and discipline.

To arm without weapons.
There is no greater catastrophe than to underestimate the enemy.
To underestimate the enemy might entail the loss of my treasures.

Rather than relying on strength and an abundance of resources, it is far better to use a superior strategy. It's also a reminder against overconfidence. The strength of an adversary must be evaluated accurately to design the correct response and optimum method of engagement.

Therefore when two equally matched armies meet,
It is the man of sorrow who wins.

*Of two opponents of roughly equal strength, the one who assumes the worst case (**"sorrow"**) will overcome the hasty arrogant one.*

IN a way, concepts of camouflage and related behavior in the conflict are applicable in trading. Demonstrating real intentions is not something large traders influencing the market want to do. While some aspects of camouflage are not directly related to a retail trader's behavior, it is very useful for him to understand these concepts as they open an insight into how influential market participants operate. Other aspects are directly applicable for a retail trader too.

Assuming that an adversary is stronger than you is the only way to proceed when electing your strategy in the market. Never try to out-stubborn it or push it with your own buying or selling. Even a small time trader sometimes feels like he can influence a relatively thin stock with his orders. It is never a good idea – liquid names can't be pushed by your buy or sell, and illiquid ones are treacherous and likely to absorb your push and turn around to rob you. If, however, you play your cards right, you may be able to take advantage of the way they move.

There is the maxim of military strategists;
I dare not be the first to invade, but rather be the invaded.

An astute trader won't engage on the market's terms – he will insist on his own terms. In practice, it means that he will enter his positions at favorable prices and specific situations, not those that the market offers him.

As lucrative as opening a long trade during a rapid upward movement may seem, such chasing is an impulsive way to trade and can be likened to "**invading**." Running higher and higher under the pressure of buying orders sent by emotional traders that fear missing the move, the market invites such "intruders" into its territory. Such hot pursuit rarely ends well for the price chasers – turnaround comes suddenly and leads to a vicious price drop. Examine any movement with strong momentum, and you no doubt will observe this phenomenon.

Meanwhile, an experienced trader, knowing how momentum trades work, will refuse to enter long positions during a parabolic movement. Controlling his emotions he will dismiss the feeling of urgency, of "missing the train." Instead, he would "***rather be the invaded***" – wait for a pullback and seek to open his position when overzealous chasers are dumping their shares in the panic caused by a sharp reversal. He will observe patiently, looking to spot the trend line and support level, project the likely depth of a pullback and wait for a confirmation. The signs he wants to see for entering the trade are:

- A parabolic spike with high volume indicating orders chasing the market,
- reversal after absorbing immense buying,
- sharp drop making buyers nervous and scaring them into liquidating their positions,
- price hitting support level created by trend lines, moving averages, recent breakout level etc, whatever indications a trader uses to read the movement,
- a pause near support level and reversal.

Seeing all these conditions, a Taoist Trader knows he has a high probability trade – getting the market where he wanted it; he can play on his own terms.

Dare not press forward an inch, but rather retreat a foot.

This line reminds us to stay patient and avoid hasty action. Looking for a long entry during upward momentum, let the pullback fully form and provide you with the best price possible. Looking for a long entry during strong downward momentum, let the reversal fully form so you are not trying to catch the falling knife. Do not feel that you must enter your trade right away – that's likely your emotions talking. Opportunities abound in the market, and your first, last and utmost consideration is the risk. The best opportunity to take is the one where you can minimize risk – leave it to the emotional crowds to chase hot prospects with no regard for danger.

That is, to march without formations,
To roll not up the sleeves,
to charge not in frontal attacks,
To arm without weapons.

This stanza describes the way for a large market player to play his cards. We need to know how they operate so we can decipher their intentions and take the right side of the market.

Let's examine two different time frames – very short, intraday one, and longer term.

Day traders have real time tools allowing them to see orders entered by other market participants – Level 2 for the stocks market is the best example of such a tool. Knowing well that his order can be seen by everyone, a participant wishing to move a large amount of shares will never display his whole order. He realizes that if a 100,000 shares buy flashes among 100 -300 shares orders, everyone will try to front-run him, and sellers will back away feeling that they can command better price. The only way for him to accumulate that many shares without putting the price out of sight is to mask his real intentions ("***march without formations***. He may buy some offers, put in some bids but those bids will never demonstrate the true scale of his intended buy. But wait, haven't we seen such big orders now and then among smaller ones, obviously standing out and attracting a lot of attention? Of course we did. Think of why the player advertised it if it could only push the market in the opposite direction and the answer becomes patently obvious – he WANTED the market to move in that direction. If he was accumulating big shares for a long position, he would most likely display a big OFFER, not the BID. That would scare smaller fish into selling – right into his hands. His real buy order size on other hand would be hidden behind reserve bid, showing small shares but absorbing all that sellers were willing to give to him. If his fake sell order wouldn't intimidate enough traders into dumping their shares, he could even turn into a seller himself and push the price down a bit to ignite more selling. Think of this phenomenon to remember once again how taking the obvious direction is not the way to go in the markets. To test this assumption in practice and make sure that a large order sticking out among smaller ones is indeed a fake, observe how it acts when threatened with actual execution. Fake order will try to stay a little away from the inside market, to be visible but not immediately liable for execution should someone decide to take it up. When hit with small orders, it will be canceled and re-entered away from the market again. Real order will just stay there and absorb all the orders executed against it.

Institutional traders accumulating a position for a longer term trade must be careful of displaying his intentions as well. We discussed it earlier when analyzing cycles of market movement. To keep his purpose under wraps for the time being, he will have "***to charge not in frontal attacks.***" Had he tried to buy everything he needs in a single day, his orders would skyrocket the price. What he will try to do is of course buy slowly and quietly, without attracting unwanted attention. Volume will increase very slowly, as our large buyer will be careful not to exceed average volume by much. It is this first stage of accumulation, when price and volume rise very slowly that is the hardest to detect (by design of course) and is the best time to take position on the large player side. Now, think of what happens when that player, having successfully accumulated a hefty position, stops masquerading and shows his hand? What purpose could he possibly have in mind? Why, to inspire the buying by the public of course. He needs their enthusiasm to propel the price up and to have buyers for his shares amassed at the lower prices. Again, as in case with intraday trading, we see that displayed intention is most likely a false one.

There is no greater catastrophe than to underestimate the enemy.
To underestimate the enemy might entail the loss of my treasures.

In light of the above, think of upgrades and downgrades by large banks, brokers and boutique firms. As market participants themselves, what interest could they possibly pursue labeling the company stocks with buy or sell recommendations? It's difficult to imagine that, intending to accumulate shares in a certain company, they would issue a strong buy alert creating competition for themselves and depriving themselves of the opportunity to buy at the lower price. Equally unlikely are they to put a sell recommendation on a stock before they liquidate their own holdings. If they are stuck in a losing position and seek an opportunity to get out at the best price possible, they are likely to issue a buy alert. Publicizing such advice, they will first and foremost take care of their financial interest. Underestimating their willingness and motivation to pursue their own financial objectives will "***entail the loss of your treasures.***"

Therefore when two equally matched armies meet,
It is the man of sorrow who wins.

Here again we are reminded about risk control as a paramount priority for a trader. Assuming the worst case scenario ("***sorrow***"), a Taoist Trader stays prepared for it. He incorporates his risk control in his actions (reasonable position size, assumption that any trade can turn sour, incorporating pre-planned stop loss on his strategy), thus no adverse development comes as a surprise for him and cause losses exceeding what his trading system allows.

71.
Sick-Mindedness

Who knows that he does not know is the highest;
Who (pretends to) know what he does not know is sick-minded.
And who recognizes sick-mindedness as sick-mindedness
is not sick-minded.
The Sage is not sick-minded.
Because he recognizes sick-mindedness as sick-mindedness,
Therefore he is not sick-minded.

Who knows that he does not know is the highest;
Who (pretends to) know what he does not know is sick-minded.

Sick-mindedness for Lao Tzu is a common condition, regularly appearing in those considered normal by society's standards. It's a man's refusal to admit the limits of his capabilities and attempt to operate beyond those limits. One of the main reasons for this tendency is pride. It motivates us to engage in conversations in which the participants have little knowledge of a subject and fail to appreciate its complexity, yet speak with great confidence as if they know what they are talking about. It stands behind the oft-seen phenomenon of "arm-chair experts"- amateurs criticizing a professional performance in any given field, be it sports, arts, science or law.

Unchecked desires push us to lose sight of the border between reality and fantasy. A healthy mind is able to make a distinction between them. In day-to-day life differentiating can often be difficult as fantasies inadvertently enter our mind in the form of unrealistic beliefs and shallow understanding.

And who recognizes sick-mindedness as sick-mindedness
is not sick-minded.
The Sage is not sick-minded.
Because he recognizes sick-mindedness as sick-mindedness,
Therefore he is not sick-minded.

To cure a condition, it must first be recognized as such. It requires strong mental discipline and humility. It also can not be cured permanently, once and for all – it's a process that stays with us throughout our entire life, so we must stay on guard for the weakness to re-appear. Our strengths will always be our strengths, as will our weaknesses always be our weaknesses.

Who knows that he does not know is the highest;
Who (pretends to) know what he does not know is sick-minded.

For a trader, this is a familiar sight: groups of online forum participants and bloggers discussing all kinds of intricacies in various fields of activity. No matter what their profession is, they suddenly become experts in anything that their beloved companies do – gold mining, shipment, oil extraction, manufacturing of electronic components, banking, car design and drug trials. A trader trying to find out what happens with a company in whose stock he is interested, will be offered extensive advice by complete strangers claiming deep knowledge and expressing absolute confidence in their views. Many of them gained their "knowledge" from online articles or popular literature; not having professional training they have no criteria by which to evaluate the information. Yet they feel qualified to argue points and give investment advice based on such understanding.

Worse yet, many of such "researchers" fail to appreciate the divide between company prospects and stock performance. Thus their findings, even if correct, may have very little to do with the only subject that ultimately makes or breaks the trade – price change of the stock. Aside from the product or technology, there are many other factors influencing market behavior: financial state of the company, competition, shares issuance, company indebtness, sources of financing, marketing skills, leadership skills etc etc. There are numerous examples of catastrophic errors in judgment made by home-grown experts in every conceivable industry. Company working on wearable computers and labeled as "the next Microsoft" becomes a darling of the technophiles and their "retirement nest egg" (actual quote from their claims), only to fade away a few short years later. Gold exploration in Indonesia gives a meteoric rise to a company claming to discover a huge field, and overzealous investors become experts in reading geological maps and analyzing nuances of foreign politics – all to end in a huge fraud scandal. Fuel cell technology promising to become a solution to oil problems send a stock skyrocketing, only to see it abandoning the idea in a few years with stock price trading at a fraction of former highs. Endless stories of miracle cures for devastating diseases, amazing inventions in all thinkable fields of activity, technologies reshaping the world lure naïve investors into eternal trap of hope – a trap whose very existence is possible thanks to their overconfidence and refusal to understand and accept their limits. All these examples illustrate fantasies flooding our mind and replacing the reality.

All this does not lead us to a conclusion that a trader should abandon research altogether. A Taoist Trader, however, understands his inherent limitations and humbly accepts them. He will not fall into the trap of arrogance, making him think of himself as a know-it-all. He will appreciate the fact that he does not possess professional knowledge in all sectors and industries and can't make competent judgments. That doesn't mean, however, that he is incapable of finding the most probable direction of price movement. So, how can he do it and what does research mean to him?

As an experienced trader with a deep understanding of the markets knows how available information and price interact with each other. This is the major weapon in a trader's arsenal and this is exactly the area of a Taoist Trader's expertise. This is where his professional knowledge lies.

So, applying what he knows about this subject, he will absorb whatever information is being revealed to the public and observe the price action against the backdrop of such information. Armed with an understanding of Taoist principles in the marketplace, he will conclude that:

- slow price rise and careful volume increase without any available news or encouraging information means that such information is upcoming, and it's time to initiate a position in preparation for that time;
- positive optimistic information being announced loudly and propagated widely with sharp price rise means that the end of the upward movement is close, and it's time to liquidate his long position and start looking for a short entry;
- positive information disseminated everywhere accompanied by a price stall and/or beginning of decline means that information is fully priced in and it's time for a short entry;
- negative information freely available not leading to a price decline means that information is fully priced in and it's time to look for a long entry.

As you can see, the common theme in this approach is to judge the information by a proxy. A Taoist Trader is interested not so much in the information itself (he knows he can't evaluate it properly) as he is in how this information is reflected in market action. This is something he can judge and use to base his decisions. This is how, to use some recent examples, an astute trader knew to short the market after TARP was approved in the fall of 2008 (market failed to advance when it became clear that the approval will be gained, and crashed right after the votes came in), or to go long and stay long in the late spring/summer of 2009 (when the market was rising from the march lows despite negative predictions everywhere).

A Taoist Trader, avoiding what he recognizes as sick-mindedness, will always humbly accept the limits to his knowledge. He will focus on his area of expertise and practice his skills instead of arrogantly overextending himself and pretending to be an expert in everything.

SUPPLEMENTARY CHAPTERS

19. Realize the Simple Self

Banish wisdom, discard knowledge,
And the people shall profit a hundredfold;
Banish "humanity," discard "justice,"
And the people shall recover love of their kin;
Banish cunning, discard "utility,"
And the thieves and brigands shall disappear.
As these three touch the externals and are inadequate,
The people have need of what they can depend upon:
Reveal thy simple self,
Embrace thy original nature,
Check thy selfishness,
Curtail thy desires.

"**Banishing wisdom and discarding knowledge**" of course refers to a false knowledge. Taoism addresses two kinds of such fake wisdom. One is impractical useless musings about things and concepts irrelevant to the task at hand and possibly lying beyond our capacities for comprehension – often referred to as "mental masturbation". Another is misinformation and artificial values imposed by societal structures. A trader is constantly subjected to propaganda by numerous entities with their own agenda; misinformation is disseminated via various channels. None of the market participants place anyone's interests at heart before their own; a Taoist Trader knows this and compares their advice (some money manager on CNBC says, "buy this stock now!") to price action (the stock has been in a parabolic rise for the last month – don't buy!) to find instances where he can position himself to utilize the propaganda ("**profit a hundredfold**") instead of being its victim.

Reveal thy simple self,
Embrace thy original nature,
Check thy selfishness,
Curtail thy desires.

A Taoist Trader keeps his approach simple and robust. The desire to overcomplicate a trading system by multiple complex technical indicators is Ego-driven as it makes a trader feel as though he belongs to some sophisticated league or gives him false feeling of being more in control. In reality they cloud his thinking more than they help. Clarity comes from "**embracing original nature**" – deep understanding how major market moving forces interact and reveal themselves in price and volume. A wise trader knows the limits of his knowledge and abilities, stays humble ("**checks his selfishness**") and keeps his feet on the ground, pursuing realistic targets and focusing on making the right trade instead of making money ("**curtailing his desires**")

21. Manifestations of Tao

The marks of great Character
Follow alone from the Tao.The thing that is called Tao
Is elusive, evasive.
Evasive, elusive,
Yet latent in it are forms.
Elusive, evasive,
Yet latent in it are objects.
Dark and dim,
Yet latent in it is the life-force.
The life-force being very true,
Latent in it are evidences.

From the days of old till now
Its Named (manifested forms) have never ceased,
By which we may view the Father of All Things.
How do I know the shape of the Father of All Things?
Through these (manifested forms)!

Major underlying principles govern all market movements, just as Tao governs the development of all things. Those principles manifest themselves through the prints on the tape, bars or candles on the charts and volume matching each print or bar. As simple and open to anyone to see, they are nonetheless "**evasive, elusive**" – they can be analyzed via their manifestations but not perceived directly. These principles explain how and why the obvious way cannot be the right way to act in the market; how the minority profits from the emotional actions of the majority; how an individual trader can spot such opportunities and position himself on the right side.

In these manifestations a Taoist Trader can discern "**forms**" – familiar patterns and situations; "**objects**" – market participants and the vehicles they use to achieve their purposes. He also understands that "**latent**" in those principles is the very "**life-force**" of the market – market exists thanks to these very principles, for if the obvious action was right action, everyone would do it and the price would never move anywhere at all – no one would be selling at $20 or buying at $40 if it were obvious that the "right" price is $30. Uncertainties, impossibility to obtain all the information create the room for opinions instead of firm knowledge, thus opening doors to differences in outlook. Such differences lead to transaction – buys and sells, prints on the tape, price changes. Since those are merely opinions, there is also room for ego, emotions and irrational actions. Thus, the very existence of the market is possible thanks to those governing principles, and they reveal themselves in the market actions ("**Its Named (manifested forms) have never ceased, By which we may view the Father of All Things.**") No matter what particular trading vehicle we look at – tulips, stocks, oil contracts – or what time we discuss – era of teletype prints, phone orders or warring computer algorithms – the underlying principles remain the same. It is technical details and particularities that change.

23. Identification with Tao

Nature says few words:
Hence it is that a squall lasts not a whole morning.
A rainstorm continues not a whole day.
Where do they come from?
From Nature.
Even Nature does not last long (in its utterances),
How much less should human beings?

Therefore it is that:
He who follows the Tao is identified with the Tao.
He who follows Character (Teh) is identified with Character.
He who abandons (Tao) is identified with abandonment (of Tao).
He who is identified with Tao –
Tao is also glad to welcome him.
He who is identified with character –
Character is also glad to welcome him.
He who is identified with abandonment –
Abandonment is also glad to welcome him.
He who has not enough faith
Will not be able to command faith from others.

The first stanza can be read as a warning that no market phenomenon lasts forever; a trader must remember that and stay nimble, knowing that he should be on the lookout for change and must cease his participation before it's too late ("**Even Nature does not last long, How much less should human beings?** "). Well-known traders' sayings highlight this approach: "sell when you can, not when you have to;" "first and last 1/8 are the most expensive" (this last one comes from the times when market was trading in fractions), "feed them when they quack"etc, including my personal favorite: "Sell the peanuts when the circus is in town, because when the circus leaves who are you going to sell your peanuts to."

The second stanza is a Taoist way of saying: in the market, everyone gets what he deserves, where deserving is determined by the degree one's actions match Taoist principles. If a trader acts in accordance with underlying market laws and patterns, controls his risk and keeps his emotions in check, the Tao will be "**glad to welcome him**." Equally, a trader allowing his mind to become confused, losing clarity of thought, not accepting reality and letting his emotions take control abandons Tao, and **abandonment** will also be "**glad to welcome him**."

This message may sound harsh and ruthless (and it is – remember, "**Nature is unkind, it treats the myriad things like straw dogs**"), but at the same time, as is always the case with Taoism, there is a bright side. If both Tao and abandonment are willing to "**welcome us**," then it's entirely up to us to choose the right way, to condition and train ourselves, and follow the path outlined by correctly understanding of the market. Proper conduct will be rewarded by achieving desired results.

25. The Four Eternal Models

Before the Heaven and Earth existed
There was something nebulous:
Silent, isolated,
Standing alone, changing not,
Eternally revolving without fail,
Worthy to be the Mother of All Things.
I do not know its name
And address it as Tao.
If forced to give it a name, I shall call it "Great."
Being great implies reaching out in space,
Reaching out in space implies far-reaching,
Far-reaching implies reversion to the original point.

• • •

Man models himself after the Earth;
The Earth models itself after Heaven;
The Heaven models itself after Tao;
Tao models itself after nature.

Major principles governing market movements are profoundly simple yet remarkably resistant to summarization. It's practically impossible to come up with a single-sentence definition unless it's something as unhelpful as "the market is what the market is." However, going over this book, you adopted a certain way of thinking. Looking at the market and trading through the Taoist system of beliefs can be extremely satisfying and rewarding. Intuitively it feels like a primal order of things – which it is. The laws governing the market are the same laws that govern Nature. They are basic and rule everything – any variation, any novelty or alteration happens within the framework of those laws. It can be very tempting sometimes to think of a certain condition as something never seen before and not fitting into any known chain of events. In reality, such a feeling is nothing but weakness – the desire to forfeit responsibility for the outcome of a trader's actions. Any "new" development will fit into patterns known to a trader if he looks at them through the prism of the Taoist philosophy. The most common example of such behavior is resignation in the face of real or alleged market manipulation. A Trader concedes his ability to extract profit from the market claiming that manipulators distort market actions. In reality, interventionists and manipulators of all kinds do not operate in a vacuum or on a whim. They have their interests and purposes – thus their actions can be deciphered and exploited.

Last stanza of this poem puts the model for a Taoist Trader in succinct form. Tao is modeled after Nature. Market, being part of life, is modeled by the same principles. To be in tune with market patterns, a trader must align his behavior with Taoist principles.

26. Heaviness and Lightness

The Solid is the root of the light;
The Quiescent is the master of the Hasty.Therefore the Sage travels all day
Yet never leaves his provision-cart.
In the midst of honor and glory,
He lives leisurely, undisturbed.

How can the ruler of a great country
Make light of his body in the empire (by rushing about)?
In light frivolity, the Center is lost;
In hasty action, self-mastery is lost.

Firm grasp on the market laws and patterns allows a trader to act with seeming ease, in the natural flow. Quiet calm allows him to stay composed in the middle of the frenzied action. He may look at any market sector but will choose his trades within his zone of comfort dictated by his risk tolerance and setups he knows and trades regularly. Whatever frantic activity takes place, he won't allow events to drawn him in; he will remain in control of his action and will engage on his terms and when he feels comfortable. A Taoist Trader knows that temptation from fast and furious action promising fast and easy riches is very deceptive; yielding to such a siren voice leaves a trader with no control, vulnerable to powers exceeding what he can handle. Losing his ability to control risk, he can experience losses much larger than what he can afford.

27. On Stealing the Light

• • •

Therefore the good man is the Teacher of the bad.
And the bad man is the lesson of the good.

He who neither values his teacher
Nor loves the lesson
Is one gone far astray.

• • •

A Taoist Trader dismisses neither losing traders around him as useless. Their errors serve as a constant reminder of erroneous ways so he can keep himself in check ("**bad man is the lesson of the good**"). Recognizing the flaws in their thoughts and actions, he can use them as an insight into the behavior of the masses. Knowing how the majority acts, he gains a good idea of how the masses view the market at any given moment. It gives him a clue how to position himself.

Interacting with those in close proximity, he may impart his understanding. He, however, will never insist on it and try to make others view things his way. He knows the Taoist way of thinking is not for the masses; he realizes that it's up to a listener to recognize the truth in his words. One who can't or won't hear it is the one "**who neither values his teacher, Nor loves the lesson** and **Is one gone far astray.**"

Another application of this last stanza is a Taoist Trader's perception of losses. He values them as lessons; a well-controlled loss will not cause much damage to his trading account but may give him a signal that his actions are incorrect. He will carefully look into each losing trade to determine whether it was a loss caused by simple odds or by a mistake of his own making. Spotting a pattern of losses in a certain repeated situation, he will make corrections to eliminate such losses. Acting this way, he "**values his teacher** and **loves the lesson.**"

28. Keeping to the Female

He who is aware of the Male
But keeps to the Female
Becomes the ravine of the world.
Being the ravine of the world,
He has the original character which is not cut up.
And returns again to the (innocence of the) babe.

He who is conscious of the white (bright)
But keeps to the black (dark)
Becomes the model for the world.
Being the model for the world,
He has the eternal power which never errs,
And returns again to the Primordial Nothingness.

He who is familiar with honor and glory
But keeps to obscurity
Becomes the valley of the world.
Being the valley of the world,
He has an eternal power which always suffices,
And returns again to the natural integrity of uncarved wood.

Break up this uncarved wood
And it is shaped into vessel
In the hands of the Sage
They become the officials and magistrates.
Therefore the great ruler does not cut up.

All the motives of this poem are well familiar to a reader by now. They are expressed in a very poetic elegant form here and it's a pure pleasure to re-read it and briefly review those concepts.

Being "**aware of the Male**" but "**keep(ing) to the Female**" refers to man's natural inclination to focus on the material things (yang) while neglecting somewhat the seemingly immaterial yet more important things (yin). In trading it can refer to focusing on profits and losses as opposed to the process itself. The individual/trader needs to strengthen and harmonize both the yin and yang character within themselves and their activities.

This principle also refers to having a strong foundation of logical thinking but being also capable of listening to intuition. A robust system of beliefs allows a trader to analyze situation and outline the best course of action. Intuition allows high efficiency and instantaneous decision making.

"**Original character**" and "**innocence of the babe**" refers to staying true to the natural laws and patterns instead of artificial values and beliefs. For a trader, it means focusing on the principal laws governing market behavior, instead of propaganda disseminated by entities with agendas.

Being "**conscious of the white**" but "**keep(ing) to the black**" puts a trader in harmony with the natural cycle of the rise and fall of the Opposites, thus he becomes a "**model for the world**" where Opposites eternally fluctuate and unite in Oneness.

A trader "**familiar with honor and glory**" but "**keep(ing) to obscurity**" makes a conscious effort not to act in a way attracting too much attention, arguments and competition. He views attempts to obtain recognition as vain and a waste of time. **Honor and glory** for the trader is money and what it can bring. **Obscurity** is humility and process. You can't have the former, or keep it, without maintaining the latter.

32. Tao is Like the Sea

Tao is absolute and has no name.
Though the uncarved wood is small,
It cannot be employed (used as vessel) by anyone.
If kings and barons can keep (this unspoiled nature),
The whole world shall yield them lordship of their own accord.

The Heaven and Earth join,
And the sweet rain falls,
Beyond the command of men,
Yet evenly upon all.

Then human civilization arose and there were names.
Since there were names,
It were well one knew where to stop.
He who knows where to stop
May be exempt from danger.
Tao in the world
May be compared to rivers that run into the sea.

Once again we are reminded that the primary market laws determine all happenings. Any change in price and volume is a manifestation of those laws. No intervention in the natural flow of things can alter the market course for too long ("**cannot be employed (used as vessel) by anyone**"); at some point the action will reverse and return to the normal track, destroying the artificial changes introduced by "**kings and barons**." Artificially supported markets will inevitably crash when the support is withdrawn, and the scale of the crash is likely to be significantly larger than it would have been should there be no intervention. A skillful trader seeing signs of manipulation will analyze the interests on the interventionist and exploit the movement caused by his actions. He will also watch for signs of the market reversing to its "**unspoiled nature**" to determine his further action.

The market carries equal opportunity for each and every participant. Moving in accordance with laws that can be studied and internalized by any trader, it offers chance to profit "**evenly upon all**."

"He who knows where to stop
May be exempt from danger" – if by now you can't think immediately of three applications for this stanza, start the book from the beginning.

Manifesting itself in each and every market movement, the laws governing the market ("**Tao in the world**) can be deduced from those very movements. Thus, every occurrence or pattern is like "**rivers that run into the sea**"- part of those laws, their expression; they can be analyzed using the understanding of the laws and they can serve as a tool for analyzing the laws themselves.

Upon reading this poem and its trading application, let's insert another one out of turn here, as its idea is very close:

34. The Great Tao Flows Everywhere

The Great Tao flows everywhere,
(Like a flood) it may go left or right.
The myriad things derive their life from it,
And it does not deny them.
When its work is accomplished,
It does not take possession.
It clothes and feeds the myriad things,
Yet does not claim them as its own.
Often (regarded) without mind or passion,
It may be considered small.
Being the home of all things, yet claiming not,
It may be considered great.
Because to the end it does not claim greatness,
Its greatness is achieved.

33. Knowing Oneself

He who knows others is learned;
He who knows himself is wise.
He who conquers others has power of muscles;
He who conquers himself is strong.
He who is contented is rich.
He who is determined has strength of will.
He who does not lose his center endures.
He who dies yet (his power) remains has long life.

Understanding the behavior of market participants is a necessary element of learning to trade. Understanding oneself, however, is even more important and in fact is crucial for successful trading. Knowing one's strength and weaknesses is vital for cultivating self-control. A wise trader knows what situations can trigger erroneous behavior; he consciously designs methods of self-discipline and learns to keep himself in check ("**conquers himself**.") Trader Routines appendix in the end of this book will help a reader with recognizing such situations and preparing for them.

36. The Rhythm of Life

He who is to be made to dwindle (in power)
Must first be caused to expand.
He who is to be weakened
Must first be made strong.
He who is to be laid low
Must first be exalted to power.
He who is to be taken away from
Must first be given,
– This is the Subtle Light.Gentleness overcomes strength:
Fish should be left in the deep pool,
And sharp weapons of the state should be left
Where none can see them.

First part of the poem is a warning about the danger of pride and reminder about inevitable cycles of life. Expansion carries seeds of contraction; gain of strength leads to weakening; rise to power is a prelude to a downfall.

"**Gentleness**" in Taoist texts is adaptation, flexibility. Flexible being able to survive through changing shape, bending and adapting, while strong and firm breaks under force, is a major Taoist theme. This is an appropriate time to cite another poem of Tao Te Ching speaking to this concept, and the motives of this poem will be no doubt very familiar to you:

76. Hard and Soft

When man is born, he is tender and weak;
At death, he is hard and stiff.
When the things and plants are alive, they are soft
and supple;
When they are dead, they are brittle and dry.
Therefore hardness and stiffness are the companions of death,
And softness and gentleness are the companions of life.

Therefore when an army is headstrong, it will lose in a battle.
When a tree is hard, it will be cut down.
The big and strong belong underneath.
The gentle and weak belong at the top.

41. Qualities of the Taoist

When the highest type of men hear the Tao (truth),
they try hard to live in accordance with it.
When the mediocre type hear the Tao,
they seem to be aware and yet unaware of it.
When the lowest type hear the Tao,
They break into loud laughter –
If it were not laughed at, it would not be Tao.

Therefore there is the established saying:
"Who understands Tao seems dull of comprehension;
Who is advance in Tao seems to slip backwards;
Who moves on the even Tao (Path) seems to go up and down."

Superior character appears like a hollow (valley);
Sheer white appears like tarnished;
Great character appears like infirm;
Pure worth appears like contaminated.
Great space has no corners;
Great talent takes long to mature;
Great music is faintly heard;
Great form has no contour;
And Tao is hidden without a name.
It is this Tao that is adept at lending (its power)
and bringing fulfillment.

First lines of this poem give us description of the stages of trader's development. A wise trader knows the value of the primary laws dictating the market events and does everything possible to coordinate his actions with these laws ("**try hard to live in accordance with it**.") A developing trader is "**aware of it**" but for the most part finds it too difficult to follow the disciplined procedures in practice. A member of the "trading masses" can't grasp the reality of these laws and denies their existence ("**break(s) into loud laughter**.") The market can function as it does exactly because of this inability of the majority to understand, appreciate and follow these underlying laws ("**it were not laughed at, it would not be Tao**.") Just as Taoism is a philosophy for the individual rather than for the masses, trading rules – as simple and profound as they are – can't be adopted and followed by the majority of market participants.

A Taoist Trader, in his quest for clarity and simplicity disregards a large part of the body of knowledge commonly considered necessary for trading. He dismisses TV channels, newsletters and the endless flow of opinions expressed in numerous blogs and articles. In conversation with pundits well versed in seemingly useful information he may seem "**dull of comprehension**." Knowing the uncertain nature of the market and understanding the limitations of human ability to analyze it, he will sound rather unsure when asked about future direction ("**Great character appears like infirm**.") Many participants of market-related discussions are driven by emotions, thus experience and express anger about influential market players, blaming them for their losses. A Taoist Trader knows that those powerful figures are a part of the market structure and must be incorporated in one's read of future direction. Not labeling things as "good" and "evil" and staying emotionally detached to preserve the clarity of his thinking, he does not share strong negative feelings toward "manipulators;" thus, he may be perceived as siding with them ("**Pure worth appears like contaminated**.")

43. The Softest Substance

The softest substance of the world
Goes through the hardest.
That-which-is-without-form penetrates that-which-has-no-crevice;
Through this I know the benefit of taking no action.
The teaching without words
And the benefit of taking no action
Are without compare in the universe.

Knowledge, deep understanding and humility ("**softest substance**") allows a Taoist Trader to succeed against the brutal force of the powerful financial behemoths. He never takes them head on; instead he uses his understanding of the way they operate to take advantage of the effects.

Second part of the poem is yet another reminder about the power and benefits of non-interference (We Wei).

Similar motive involving classic Taoist reference, water, can be seen in Poem

78. Nothing Weaker than Water:

There is nothing weaker than water
But none is superior to it in overcoming the hard,
For which there is no substitute.
That weakness overcomes strength
And gentleness overcomes rigidity,

You can refer to **Chapter 8. Water** for more trading applications.

45. Calm Quietude

The highest perfection is like imperfection,
And its use is never impaired.
The greatest abundance seems meager,
And its use will never fail.
What's most straight appears devious,
The greatest skill appears clumsiness;
The greatest eloquence seems like stuttering.
Movement overcomes cold,
(But) keeping still overcomes heat.
Who is calm and quiet becomes the guide for the universe.

This series of contrasts is very typical for Taoist thinking and by now should be very familiar and even comfortable for a reader. The purest form of market forces manifestation (movement against the obvious) seems very illogical to an inexperienced trader ("**The highest perfection is like imperfection.**"). In the same fashion, trading decisions made by an astute trader look irrational to the trading masses. In fact, this can be one of his measuring tools to evaluate his idea – if the majority around agrees with him, he will become suspicious of his own plan. This is not out of pure contrarian thinking no matter what – rather it is because he knows that the market normally does not act in a way rewarding the majority, thus finding himself on the same side with crowds he senses a danger. His straightforward thinking may strike some around him as "**devious,**" as social customs call for a more "nuanced" approach. His skills express such simplicity that, in spite of being robust, they may appear "**clumsiness.**" His words express such profound and simple truth that they may sound too simple ("**stuttering**") for those listeners who like to think of themselves as more sophisticated.

A Taoist Trader is interested in detecting the first signs of life in seemingly "dead" trading vehicles, unpopular and unknown to the trading public. It is those first signs that offer the best opportunity for early entry ("**Movement overcomes cold.**") When the action becomes overheated, he knows it's not the time to initiate a new position as Smart Money liquidates its, and it's only the unskilled masses that jump on the bandwagon that is about to reverse ("**keeping still overcomes heat.**")

If the meaning of the concluding line of this poem, "**Who is calm and quiet becomes the guide for the universe,**" is not immediately clear – start this book from the beginning, and this time really read it.

47. Pursuit of Knowledge

Without stepping outside one's doors,
One can know what is happening in the world,
Without looking out of one's windows,
One can see the Tao of heaven.

The farther one pursues knowledge,
The less one knows.
Therefore the Sage knows without running about,
Understands without seeing,
Accomplishes without doing.

A Taoist Trader bases his read of the market direction on the eternal laws, and he knows that their role in shaping events is absolute and undeniable. There are no principally new happenings that would require principally new understanding to explain them. Every "new paradigm" is just a variation of an old paradigm; if the turn of events seems "never seen before" to an observer, it's simply a testament to his, observer's, lack of familiarity with primal laws. The experienced trader notices similarities between the situation in progress and those which have come before, while unskilled one tends to see the differences and claim that something unprecedented happens. Naturally, the former can use his observations as a compass while to the latter the situation seems unmanageable.

The endless quest to find the reasons and prognoses by reading more and more articles, blogs, interviews, opinions and newsletters eventually introduces more confusion. Excessive information where personal opinions and agendas become increasingly difficult to filter out takes away clarity of thinking ("**The farther one pursues knowledge, The less one knows.**")

48. Conquering the World by Inaction

The student of knowledge (aims at) learning day by day;
The student of Tao (aims at) losing day by day.
By continual losing
One reaches doing nothing (laissez-faire).
He who conquers the world often does so by doing nothing.
When one is compelled to do something,
The world is already beyond his conquering.

There is a great paradox in learning to trade about which many accomplished traders comment when speaking about their learning process. This paradox is in contrast to studying various technical and fundamental tools and approaches on one side, and robust simplicity on another. Indeed, no one expects a beginning trader to dismiss out of hand the body of knowledge about the markets accumulated over the centuries. There are high quality books written by responsible knowledgeable authors; there are methods based on solid understanding of market nature. There is, however, a lot of drivel as well. Finally, not all meaningful approaches suit a particular trader. Thus, after the initial stage of "**learning day by day**," a "**student of knowledge**" must turn into a "**student of Tao**" and start "**losing day by day**" – discarding the knowledge that does not contribute to his effectiveness. Getting rid of numerous indicators, studies and channels of information while leaving only the simplest forms of visual aid, is a common theme for many successful traders describing their learning process. Trimming unneeded information, a Taoist Trader uses less for better results, thus achieving higher effectiveness. What is left when his actions are based on solid understanding of the Tao in the markets, discarding propaganda and doing less for better results, can be expressed in three words. Let these words conclude our course, and let them be your guide in trading:

Simple. Robust. Effective.

Appendix 1. TRADER ROUTINES

We discussed the role and use of trader routines in the Chapter 24. **The Dregs and Tumors of Virtue**. Below are a few routines designed for the most typical situations and problems a trader encounters. You don't need to use them all – they are designed to help with particular problems and need to be applied if you encounter the problem described. Go over them and see which of them may apply to you. Each routine consists of the following elements:

Situation: description of the problem behavior.

Diagnosing the problem: identification of the trigger for the problem behavior and erroneous beliefs causing it.

Philosophical foundation: brief reminder of the beliefs and concepts reinforcing correct behavior.

Routine: steps to undertake to prevent problem behavior in identified situation.

Mantra: concise short sentences to recite, helping reinforce right state of mind.

Feel free to tweak the suggested routines to your particular time frame, use them as a template to design your own, and adjust the mantras for maximum effectiveness.

1. Revenge trading.

Situation: A trader encounters a loss at the start of the day. Not willing to accept the loss, he starts pushing hard for remediation, initiating trades where there is no valid setup for them, digging the hole deeper and, again, pushing harder. As a result, the day ends with a sizeable loss, much bigger than the initial one that caused the spiral of self-destructive behavior.

Diagnosing the problem: Finding out the trigger for revenge trading – an exact number of losing trades or dollar amount of a loss that triggers the harmful behavior.

Philosophical foundation: Our knowledge is limited – we can not know all there is to know. We can not predict the future, thus there is always room for an unforeseen turn of events. It means that losses are unavoidable and a certain percentage of losing trades and days are expected. Cyclical nature of all phenomena also means that winning trades and days will take turns with losing ones. Losses are a normal, natural and inalienable part of the trading process. Not every day must be a winning one; there is no need to be alarmed by a loss and try immediately to remediate it.

Revenge Trading Prevention Routine.

1. Leave your computer for 30 minutes. Go outside, do a breathing exercise. Recite the part of your trading philosophy describing the place and role of losses in trading.

   Your mantra:

   The only reason to put on a trade is a valid setup in terms of my system. Being down for the day is not a reason to trade. The market doesn't care about my being up or down. It generates profitable opportunities every day. I wait for the market to create a situation I can recognize. I am not eager to find the trade. I will know when it comes along. I don't have to win back immediately what I lost earlier. I will win it back when the right trade comes along. I sit and wait for the right opportunity.

2. Return to your computer. Start observing market action trying to view it as a fresh start, as if your day just started.

3. Make your next three trades a paper trades. Pay special attention to the reason for the trade – make sure that your entries are based on real setups, not on wishful thinking. Staying with paper trading will give you back your discipline – discipline of stopping yourself from harmful behavior, taking back control over your action.

4. If your trades continue losing, stay with paper trading till the end of the day. If they are winning ones, start trading real money again but with half of your usual position size.

5. When you establish firm pattern of returning to setup-based trading as opposite to emotion-based right after returning to your computer, you may switch back to real trading skipping paper trading stage, but with half lot position size.

2. Blowing the Stop.

Situation: A trade starts with defined setup, including a stop level. However, if the price approaches a stop, the trader finds reason to cancel his stop convincing himself that he needs to give a trade more "breathing room." Not willing to accept the growing loss, he refuses to take it until the pain becomes unbearable. As a result, the trade ends with a sizeable loss, much bigger than the intended.

Diagnosing the problem: unwillingness to accept a loss, unrealistic desire to trade without losses, perceiving a loss as a sign of personal inadequacy.

Philosophical foundation: Our knowledge is limited – we can not predict the future, thus losses are unavoidable and a certain percentage of losing trades and days are expected. Cyclical nature of all phenomena also means that winning trades and days will take turns with losing ones. Losses are a normal, natural and inalienable part of the trading process. Stop loss is not a loss – it is prevention of a loss from growing. Stop loss is not sign of foolishness – refusal to apply it is.

Stop Loss Blowing Routine.

1. As price approaches your stop level, prepare exit order; avoid looking at the profit/loss column.

2. Think of the small loss you are about to take, saving your account from a large one.

3. Feel grateful for the concept of stop that guarantees your safety.

4. Look at the chart, envision a trade moving against you beyond the stop level and feel the fear of a loss growing uncontrollably.

5. As the stop is hit, send an exit order with great relief of getting rid of a losing trade endangering your account.

Your mantra in this routine is one you need to reread at the start of the trading day.

Stopping out prevents losses. A stop is not a loss. A stop prevents a loss from growing. I am listening to the market and doing what it tells me to do. If I find myself in the wrong place at the wrong time, it's in my power to get out. I have the responsibility to keep my trading account in good shape, and stop loss is my way to protect it. There is nothing wrong in being stopped out. A stop does not make me a loser. It makes me a winner, saving me from destruction. This is my way to control events. I want to be in control and be happy. No trade is so significant that it's worth holding onto if it doesn't work. The next opportunity comes right away. I switch easily from the trade that doesn't work to another that will. I enter any trade accepting in advance that it can stop me out. If the trade doesn't work out, it won't come as a surprise to me. My trading strategy has the inevitability of losses built into it, and no single loss can get out of hand.

3. Letting Winners Run

Situation: A trade develops in a trader's favor. However, as soon as he sees any profit, no matter how insignificant it is, he rushes to take it not letting a trade mature. Taking too small profits while keeping predetermined stops undermines overall performance.

Diagnosing the problem: fear to let profits evaporate, insecurity about trading system, intrusion in the natural development of the trade.

Philosophical foundation: Every process has its natural cycles. We need to avoid meddling with them. Ruining the ratio of win and loss size, we distort the system performance. Cutting our profits short we violate the principle of non-interference.

Letting Winners Run Routine.

1. As a trade develops in your favor, focus on the chart; avoid looking at the profit/loss column.

2. Think of the signs of the trade reaching its full potential or a threshold for partial profit-taking.

3. Observe the chart for the signs of trade exhaustion as your system defines them; ask yourself constantly whether you see them.

4. If you feel an urge to exit a trade, ask yourself why. If you have no other answer but the desire to secure profits, continue watching the action and repeatedly ask the same question as in point 3. Continue focusing on the chart and keeping inner dialog with yourself about signs of a trade exhaustion.

5. As you see confirmation of exit point reached on the chart, close the trade or take partial.

   Your mantra:

   I don't have to be right all the time. I don't have to take a profit as soon as my position shows one. I have to sell when my system generates a valid selling signal. Things once set in motion tend to remain in motion. I want to ride them while they move. My system is profit-oriented. I am going to let it generate profits. I do not interfere with natural order. The flow will take me where I need to go without effort on my part.

4. Hesitating to Pull the Trigger

Situation: A setup shapes up. Price approaches a trigger and entry signal is generated. A trader, however, hesitates to pull the trigger. Trade gets away from him as he stays frozen.

Diagnosing the problem: fear of losses, insecurity about trading system, placing too much significance in each given trade; excessive analysis generating too much worry.

Philosophical foundation: The market is uncertain – we can not predict the future, thus losses are unavoidable and a certain percentage of losing trades and days are expected. They are not to be feared as they are merely a part of the winning process. Profits are generated by the "love" from the Three Treasures: acceptance of the market as our operational environment; simple and clear choices provided by our trading system; and decisive action based on a solid proven system and discipline. Preliminary preparations in the form of strictly defined and tested setups allows us to avoid thinking through every trade anew.

Hesitation to Pull the Trigger Routine.

1. As a trade price approaches the trigger, focus on the chart and remember the elements of

the setup.

2. Consider the possible scenarios of the trade development – moving in your favor to the target and hitting your stop.

3. Play both possible scenarios in your mind and accept them as equally possible; accept that you can't predict which of them takes place on any given trade.

4. Clearly envision quick decisive action without second-guessing at the moment when entry signal is generated; watch for the signal being ready to react.

5. As the price required for your setup initiation is reached, send an entry order without thinking.

   Your mantra:

   Trading is a game of probabilities. I don't have to be right every time. I just have to follow my rules. I know my system works. Every trade is either a profit or a stop. Any given trade is not of significance. The result over a certain time period is what matters. Trading my proven system puts the odds on my side. I have to play to allow opportunities to materialize. I don't think through every trade every time – all I do is react to signals that are generated by my system. Any stock movement is simply numbers that change following certain patterns. I know how to read those patterns. I am totally focused on what the market is telling me. I hear it and react to it swiftly and decisively.

5. Overtrading

Situation: Market presents few opportunities. Waiting for the right trade takes longer than normally. A trader loses patience and starts taking impulsive trades with no proper setup.

Diagnosing the problem: impatience, false work ethics making a trader feel as if he didn't work enough to deserve the reward, striving for a stable "income."

Philosophical foundation: The market is changing constantly – there is no equality in the number of opportunities from hour to hour or day to day. Fat times yield to lean times. We must stay flexible. Our expectations should remain realistic – stable income in trading is fantasy. Money in trading is not earned by working hard – it's earned by applying the skill at the right time.

Overtrading Prevention Routine.

1. In a calm inactive market with few opportunities focus on finding the setups matching your trading system.

2. Remind yourself to stay calm and relaxed so you are ready to engage at the right time.

3. Every time you start watching a movement for possible entry, ask yourself what setup you are going to apply and remember all its elements.

4. Every time you are ready to initiate the trade, take a brief pause and ask yourself whether all the elements of the setup are present.

5. Remember that in a dull market, traditional setups are prone to fail more frequently.

   Your mantra:

   I have only one reason to put on a trade. This reason is a valid setup in terms of my system. There are no external influences that can make me trade. Boredom is not a reason to trade. Market generates profitable opportunities regardless of what I want. I wait for the market to create a situation I can recognize. I am not eager to find the trade. I will know when it comes along. I don't have to be in the market all the time. I sit and wait for the right opportunity. My money works when it's sitting on the sidelines being ready for the right moment.

For the next routine let's practice designing it on your own. Below is the description of the problem; actual routine is on the next page. Please write it yourself before going to the next page using the template of the routines above. Compare it to the one we suggest; make corrections if necessary. This exercise will prepare you for the designing your own routines in case of need.

6. Chasing the entry

Situation: A price is running fast in a vertical manner with big volume spike. Optimal entry is long gone; a trader, however, can't resist the temptation and enters near the reversal.

Diagnosing the problem: feeling that opportunity is being missed, giving in to the excitement, false hope instead of cold-blooded approach.

Philosophical foundation: The overstretched bow is about to snap – the overstretched movement is about to reverse. Every process reaches its extreme right on the verge of turning around. Parabolic hysterical movement is a sign of the majority joining in – the majority cannot be right. Entering into such a move would be accepting market terms – we need to engage on our terms by retreating and waiting for a pullback.

Chasing Prevention Routine.

1. Seeing parabolic spike in price accompanied by sharp volume increase, move away from the desk and monitor the move, reminding yourself that you are a cold-blooded observer.

2. Remind yourself to stay calm and relaxed so you are ready to engage at the right time.

3. Remind yourself that you are willing to engage on your own terms only. Wait for a pull-back offering you an entry opportunity.

4. Determine the support level where price is likely to reverse back up. Determine the signs of the bounce that will trigger your entry.

5. As the price approaches your predetermined support level, move back to your desk and prepare to send your order.

   Your mantra:

   I am a part of minority that trades against the emotional crowd. I do not join in with the crowds. I calmly wait for the price to come to me. I will take an entry when a price pulls back into support. I am not afraid of missing the profit. Opportunities are abound. I take pleasure in having steel self-control and resisting temptation of chasing.

Appendix 2. MEDITATION TECHNIQUES

Most Americans would describe meditation as the act of sitting in a relaxed position, thinking pleasant thoughts, and perhaps chanting. In short, they see meditation as really nothing more than mental entertainment. But this entertainment won't to discipline the mind and bring the benefits of concrete training. True Taoist meditation is more precisely described as a focusing exercise that employs visualization techniques to accomplish specific objectives. It uses a disciplined process of mental imagery to yield practical results. Discipline is key... Indeed, meditation is focused visualization — and it is most definitely work.

Although there are many forms of mental Chi Quong, the *Center of Traditional Taoist Studies* teaches three of the most important: (1) "emptiness," or ch'an, meditation (called "Zen" in Japan), (2) "burning" meditation, and (3) "traveling" meditation.

Emptiness meditation teaches the mind to not think and thus rid itself of thoughts, while burning meditation "burns up" the stress of daily life and helps build the immune system-it is literally the mental regimen that compliments the physical regimen.

(http://www.tao.org/mind.html)

We recommend the "**emptiness**" meditation as a way to prepare for the trading day. It should be done in the morning, about an hour before market open. Ten-fifteen minutes of this preparation can do wonders to keep a trader in a calm balanced state of mind. The "**burning**" meditation is great for after market close, to clean up your mind of the stress. "Traveling" meditation is part of the more esoteric Taoist practices and will not be included here.

Emptiness Meditation

Sit comfortably in a chair or on the floor and begin "shutting down the mind." The classic method to do so is to stare at a lit candle for a short time, allowing the image of the candle to become the primary thought in your mind. In a minute or two, close your eyes, take the image of the candle with you, and imagine yourself on a peaceful beach, with the candle sitting at your feet, and ocean's waves crashing in front of you. It is important you take the candle with you. It may help to acquire a soundtrack of Ocean surf to build the synthesis.

At this point, begin to relax your body fully. Progress through your body, concentrating on one muscle group at a time. Begin with the left big toe, command it to relax, and then continues up the left side of the body. Continuing in a similar fashion down the right side of the body, one ends with the right big toe. Each muscle in the body—even those on the face and scalp—must be fully relaxed before moving on to the next. To make sure a muscle is truly relaxed, tense it and immediately relax it. Once the body is fully relaxed, it is time to remove the flow of interfering thoughts that never leave us alone. It is a key part of mental hygiene to accomplish this through "emptiness" meditation. The art of thinking is much more difficult than it sounds. The trick in removing unwanted thoughts is to not try to halt them, but rather to simply let them go when they appear. As thoughts enter the mind, don't allow yourself to dwell on any of them. Meet each one with the greeting "later" and push it away letting them enter and pass through unhindered. For the period of meditation, thoughts come, but immediately depart. You can use the imagery of a bottomless mug where the thought enters the top of the mug and falls right through into oblivion. You may find that visualizing a piece of blank paper in your mind, on which thoughts appear that you gently push away. The point is not to not think, but to focus the thinking on one activity-being empty. As your mind settles, thoughts appear less frequently or stop altogether, and visualization of the candle and beach becomes clearer and perception of time muted. Make sure to set the alarm so you don't miss opening bell.

Burning Meditation

Start meditation as described above using emptiness mediation to relax the mind. Once this meditative state is achieved, envision drawing golden light into your body from—the candle's flame. You can inhale the light. This golden light represents healing energy that fills the body and pushes out the stress, which you will visualize as black dirt. Visualize this expelled dirt combusting upon contact with outside air and burning with a powerful, deep-red flame.

You also may visualize golden rain falling on and through your body that draws the black dirt out into a puddle at your feet that you then burn.

Continuously draw in golden light, push out the dirt of stress and burn it. Repeating this cycle several times until the visualized dirt is completely expelled, rejuvenating your mind through mental cleansing. You will feel refreshed and well-rested.

www.ingramcontent.com/pod-product-compliance
Lightning Source LLC
Chambersburg PA
CBHW061814210326
41599CB00034B/7002
9780973779653